$\mathcal{P}$RINCESS $\mathcal{M}$ARY

OF

MARYLAND

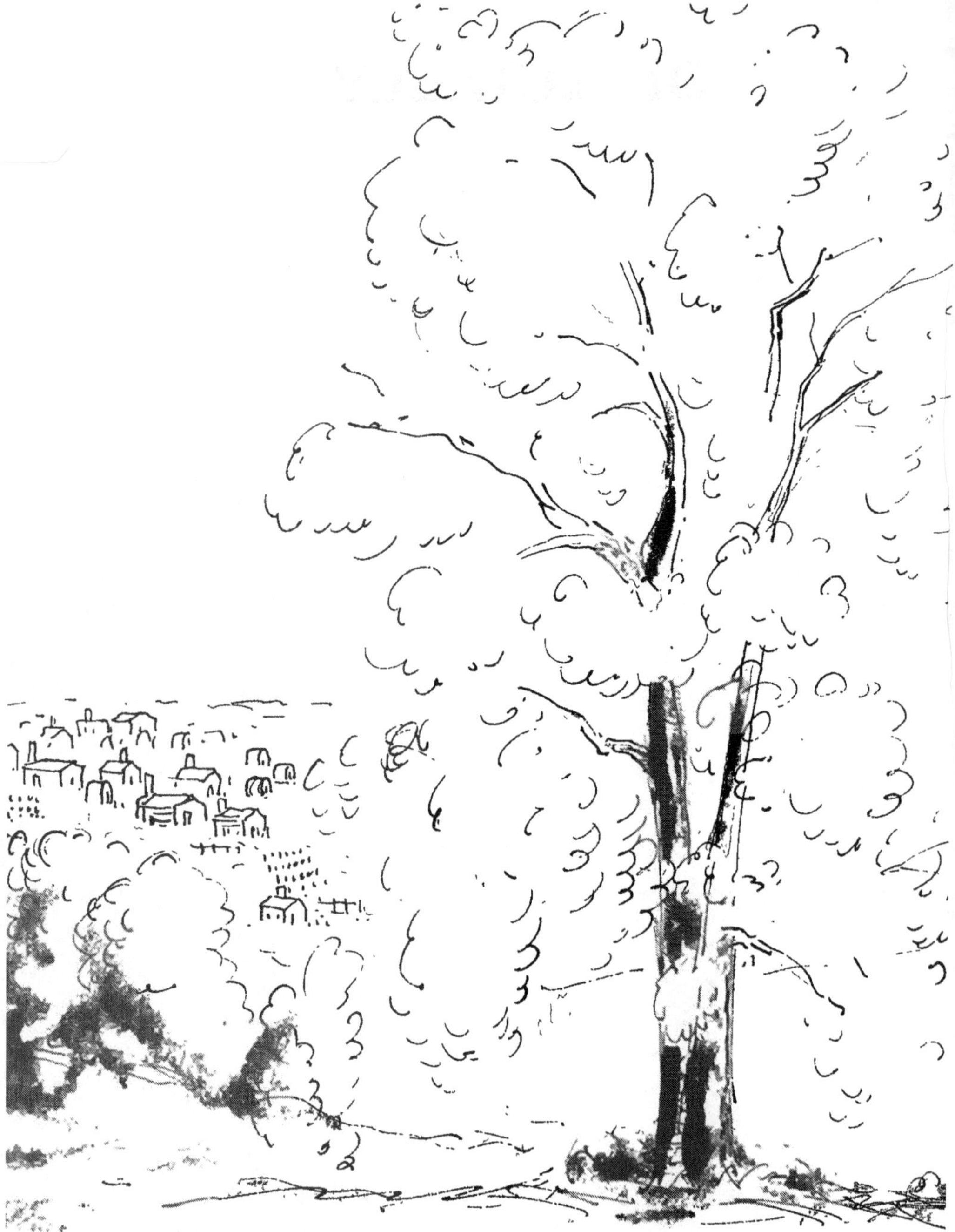
Sopher

Illustrations by Aaron Sopher

Princess

Mary

of

Maryland

by Nan Hayden Agle

CHARLES SCRIBNER'S
SONS

NEW YORK

PRINTED IN THE UNITED STATES OF AMERICA A-7.56 (R)

To Emily *and* Charles Hayden,
my mother and father

$\mathcal{A}$CKNOWLEDGMENTS

I wish to thank Eugenia Calvert Holland of the Maryland Historical Society for introducing me to Princess Mary. My father, Charles S. Hayden, who knew a great deal about Indians. Margaret Edwards and Idaline Ratcliffe for reading and criticizing the manuscript. Marjorie and Henry Woodman who lived with the Indians and know things about them not found in books.

The main sources I have used are Father Andrew White's NARRATIVE OF A VOYAGE TO MARYLAND; Elizabeth Rigby's article in the *Maryland Historical Society Magazine*, "Maryland's Royal Family"; the Chronicles of Mistress Margaret Brent; and Henry Fleet's Journal.

Contents

Princess Mary

OF
Maryland

Chapter 1

A Messenger Brings News

A LONG TIME AGO in Pascataway Village, high on a bluff overlooking the water, there lived an Indian baby named Little Girl. Around the village as far as an eagle could see there was nothing but trees—hickory, oaks straight and tall, cypress, mulberry, alder, ash, chestnut, gum, pine. And under the trees there were wild strawberries, beans, peas, and gooseberries in season. It was a good place for animals and man, with springs of fresh water to drink.

Pascataway Village lay like a patch of mushrooms near one of the springs. The houses, made of saplings bent and tied on top and covered with bark, were all alike. But the palace where Little Girl lived was larger than the rest.

A covey of partridges crossed the path to the spring, walking one behind the other. A squirrel in the tall pine by the palace door scolded pups playing under the lowest limbs.

The pups tumbled, rolled, bit and snarled like big dogs at a feast.

Little Girl, sucking on a turkey bone, toddled out of the bark palace. Her round face was covered with grease. Her chubby body, naked as a jay, glowed warm like a copper jug before the fire.

The pups sniffed, smelled meat. They bounded after Little Girl, knocked her down and ran off with the bone.

"Aya, aya, aya," she howled, "Aya."

Such a racket!

The partridges whirred into the air. The squirrel dashed to the top of the tree.

Kittamaquund, Little Girl's father, came out of the palace to see what was the matter. He was naked too, except for a narrow, fringed deerskin breechcloth which hung from a thong around his slender waist. His bronze body was lean and strong. His coarse, straight black hair was pulled back and knotted under his left ear with a dog's tooth in it for decoration.

"Aya, aya," the baby cried again.

Kittamaquund picked her up. He tossed her into the air until her cries changed to laughter. Kittamaquund's fierce black eyes burned with pride, for he loved his daughter more than anything else in the world. Other warriors wanted sons. But not Kittamaquund—Little Girl filled his heart.

Kittamaquund was an Indian brave, brother of the emperor, Uwanno, the Tayac. He was ruler of the Pascataway tribe, the Potopaco tribe, the Yaocomicoe, Chopticoe and all of the other tribes in that territory except the Anacostan.

While Kittamaquund held Little Girl, he thought of the day when he might become emperor, for he was next in line. The Indian rule was handed down from brother to sister then to the sister's children, beginning with Uttapoingassinen (founder of the royal line) a hundred years before.

If Kittamaquund were ruler, Little Girl would be princess. He looked down at her tenderly and stroked her dark hair.

All at once there was a cry overhead, "Hawn, hawn!"

"Wild geese. The first wild geese!" Kittamaquund said. "They follow the creek north. We will watch them from the bluff."

Quickly he swung the baby up on his shoulder. Fleet as a deer he ran through the narrow strip of woods that lay between the palace and the water.

A black snake slithered out of his path.

Kittamaquund and Little Girl came out on the bluff above Pascataway Creek. Below the water sparkled as it hurried on its way to the Potomac River and on to the wide Chesapeake Bay.

"Look, look, there they go!" Kittamaquund pointed to a long "V" of birds that stretched across the whole dome of heaven.

Little Girl clapped her hands, drumming her heels against her father's chest, and squealed for joy, "Tu-wee, tu-wee!" She had learned her first word from a small bird over her cradle.

When the geese faded from sight, Kittamaquund turned toward home. Suddenly he stopped. What was that? His sharp eyes spotted a motion on the water.

"Someone is coming!"

Little Girl felt his excitement and was still.

Kittamaquund watched, his muscles taut.

A canoe was coming swiftly—the paddles dip, dipping, without disturbing the surface of the water.

It came nearer and nearer. Now Kittamaquund could see that it was Nicoatucen, the messenger.

What news did he bring? Kittamaquund was eager to know but he must wait patiently.

Now the canoe was directly below. Kittamaquund watched Nicoatucen pull it up on the shore among the reeds. He watched him run swiftly up the steep bank, his dark body glistening with sweat and bear grease.

"*Quay-quay*," Kittamaquund said, greeting the messenger as he approached.

"*Quay-quay*, Kittamaquund, brother of the Tayac Uwanno. I bring news," he said, breathless with excitement. "A great canoe is coming. A canoe cut from a tree larger than any living tree. Already it has left the river and moves swiftly up the creek. It moves with great wings spread to the wind. It moves without paddles. Never have I seen such a canoe. I must go on to the emperor."

Kittamaquund was full of fear, but he must not show it.

He spoke with dignity, saying, "Go, Nicoatucen. Warn the emperor. Spread the alarm to the village." He raised his hand and Nicoatucen ran on to the village.

Kittamaquund, holding his daughter under one arm as if she were a sack of corn, followed him through the strip of woods to the palace.

Chapter 2

THE GREAT CANOE

WHEN KITTAMAQUUND entered the palace, he found his wives and Uwanno's wives weaving baskets together.

"Chew your reeds on the end," Little Girl's mother was saying. "A wet reed is easier to manage." She stopped, seeing her husband, and waited for him to speak.

Kittamaquund put Little Girl down on the hard-packed clay floor and said, "Watch the child. I have no time for her. A strange canoe is coming. I go to my brother."

"Where does the strange canoe come from?"

"Will it stop here?"

"Why is it coming?"

"Are there many people in it?"

"Are the strangers friends or enemies?" the women asked one after the other.

Kittamaquund left without answering. He had no time to bother with women and children now.

The women looked at one another apprehensively and laid aside their work.

Little Girl toddled over to a bear rug, sat down and began to play with her doll. It was a pretty doll made of deer hide and dressed like the Indian women in a doe-skin shirt and a leather skirt to the ankles.

"We need have no fear with our men to protect us," Little Girl's mother said as she stirred a savory beaver stew that was simmering on a low fire in the middle of the room. A thin wisp of smoke curled around the pot and trailed up and through the oval opening in the arched roof overhead.

The room was large. It served as living quarters for the whole family—the Tayac, his brother, and their wives and children. The emperor had a separate room with a bed to sleep on—a skin stretched on poles. Everybody else slept as soundly on mats on the floor around the fire.

"Let me help you," Uwanno's wife said to Little

Girl's mother. She filled a basket with corncobs and bones and pitched it out the open door. The dogs pounced on the bones at once. The cobs added to the clutter outdoors. But no matter, for there were two villages. When the one became unbearably dirty the tribe would move out and set up housekeeping in the second village several miles away. Then, when time, fresh air, sunlight and scavengers had picked the village clean, they would all move back again.

"Dum-dum-dum-dum," the drums sounded.

The women crowded around the door and looked out. One said, "The men are gathering. I wish someone would tell us what is going on."

Braves came out of the woods with their bows and arrows. The women drew back in fear. Little Girl's mother picked her up saying, "No harm shall come to my baby."

More drum beats—"dum-dum-dum."

The women looked out the door again in time to see the braves start toward the creek.

"Let us follow them," said one of Uwanno's wives, and the rest of the women nodded.

Little Girl's mother popped her into her *teckanagin*, her baby basket.

"You grow too big to ride on my back. You are as fat as a partridge," the mother said, teasing.

Little Girl jumped up and down and shook the sides of her basket, squealing, "Tu-wee."

"Hear her—nothing but bird talk," the women said. "When will she speak Algonquin?"

"She has been with us for only thirteen moons. Give her time. There is no hurry."

"No. But let us hurry or we'll miss the strange canoe."

Little Girl's mother swung the *teckanagin* up on her back and hung the tump line across her forehead. She walked out the palace door and the other women followed.

Little Girl loved to ride on her mother's back. It was fun to rock up and down, up and down, as her mother stepped on pine needles in her soft buckskin moccasins. She grabbed her mother's long thick braid and pulled it for fun. Her mother chuckled and shook her head.

The sun was high. A gentle breeze blew in from the water. Little Girl clapped her hands and jumped for joy as they passed through the thicket. A branch tangled in her black hair and pulled it over her eyes making her look like a shaggy bear. The women laughed at her. She shook her *teckanagin* and laughed too.

Before long they came out on a knoll overlooking the water.

The braves were gathering on the bluff nearby. A hundred or so were there already and more were coming in from neighboring villages. They looked fearsome with stern faces stained dark with walnut juice, to ward off mosquitoes and flies, and streaked with white paint from ear to chin to scare the enemy. Each warrior carried a long bow and a quiver full of arrows.

Some of the men wore deerskin cloaks swung from the shoulder, for the air was still cool, but most of them wore only the breechcloth. A few of the braves wore a single feather in their hair.

Several women came through the thicket and joined the others. They talked softly together and watched their men. Surely no enemy would dare attack such brave warriors guarding the village.

How handsome they all looked.

Kittamaquund and Uwanno were out in front of the others talking with Mosorcoques, the counselor.

The women wondered what they were saying. They hoped the talk was of peace, not of fighting.

"Little Girl, you are heavy," said her mother as she lifted the *teckanagin* from her back and hung it on a limb of a sycamore tree nearby.

Now Little Girl could see everything as she swung back and forth. She squealed.

A brave signaled for silence and the mother whispered, "Quiet, Little Girl, quiet."

By this time Little Girl was busy watching a red

ladybug with black spots which was walking slowly across her outstretched hand. Now and then the bug spread dark wings and folded them again. Little Girl had never met a ladybug before. Up, up it crawled to the tip of her tiny thumb, then away it flew. Little Girl felt joy as if she too had wings

Everybody was silent, waiting. They watched the water, listening for the slightest sound.

What was that?

Only a fish jumping out of the water, falling back with a plop.

A mockingbird sang in the top of the sycamore. He sang and sang of spring and bugs and wind in a tree.

Everyone waited. A hawk dropped from the sky. The silence was broken by a shriek of terror from some small beast among the cattails. The hawk rose again.

The shadow of the beech tree moved slowly.

There was a motion in the bushes. A naked youth, a scout, slipped silently up the steep bank and ran to Uwanno. He pointed south.

"Look," whispered the emperor's favorite wife. "The white man's canoe."

They had heard about the white man's big canoes from Captain Fleet, the explorer and trader from Jamestown. Captain Fleet was the only white man who had ever visited Pascataway Village. He visited tribes all

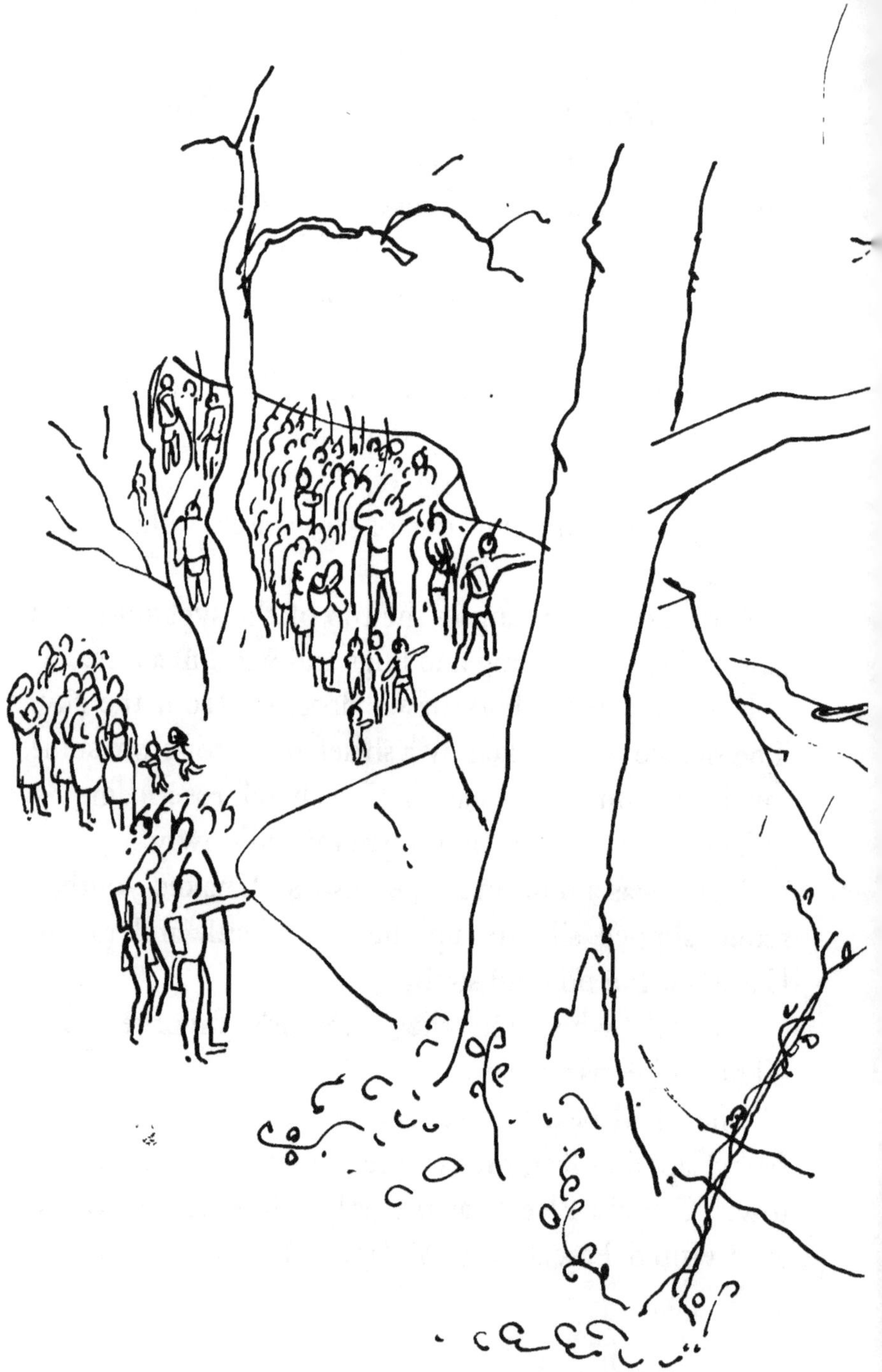

along the creeks and the rivers. Speaking both Algonquin and English, he interpreted news back and forth. He had told the English about the friendly Pascataway tribe, about Uwanno the peaceful emperor, and he had told the Pascataways about English people.

But could the white man's word be trusted? An Indian's word, yes, but what of the white man? Let him prove himself first. The warriors were uneasy as they watched the great canoe approaching. They gripped their long bows tipped with stag horns. They stood ready to fight.

The white man's canoe was a wonderful sight to see as it moved silently on the water with sails full of wind. It was wider than the palace, with two masts as tall as cypress trees.

It sailed nearer, nearer. It sailed right into the cove beneath the bluff. It lowered sails and dropped anchor.

The braves were filled with awe. They muttered together, calling upon their god, Okee, to protect them. The women drew their children closer to them in fear.

Chapter 3

A TREATY OF PEACE

*U*WANNO TURNED to Mosorcoques, the counselor, and said, "We will go to the ship and speak with the strangers."

Then Mosorcoques, Kittamaquund and Nicoatucen paddled out to the strange canoe.

The rest of the braves went down the bank and crowded together along the water's edge with their bows held ready to protect their leaders.

The women and children watched anxiously. Even Little Girl felt the tension in the air and was quiet.

Everybody watched Nicoatucen tie the canoe securely to the anchor chain of the ship. They watched the braves climb aboard.

The ship was the *Dove*, a forty-ton bark from England. The *Dove* had crossed the ocean with her sister ship, the *Ark*, bringing the first settlers to Maryland under the command of Leonard Calvert, the first governor.

When Governor Calvert heard from Captain Fleet about Uwanno, he sailed up the river in the *Dove*, leaving the *Ark* at anchor at St. Clements. And here he was, with two Jesuit priests in their black cassocks and Captain Fleet himself waiting to meet Uwanno when he and the other Indians dropped on deck. The minute Kittamaquund landed he sidled around near Governor Calvert, for never had he seen such beautiful clothes. That lace-trimmed collar and cuffs, doublet, hose and square-toed shoes and the wide-brimmed hat with a plume. Kittamaquund longed to touch them but didn't dare. He could see himself dressed in all that finery. His chest swelled at the thought. He could almost feel the soft white collar around his neck.

Uwanno raised his hand. Governor Calvert raised his in return. Uwanno stepped before the governor.

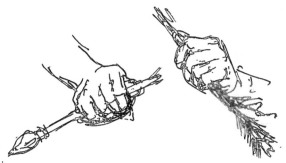

Without a word he broke an arrow in two. He took a stone axe in his hand and dulled the edge with a stone. He handed the axe and an arrow to Governor Calvert.

He too broke the arrow and dulled the axe. And with these signs peace was declared between the white man and the Pascataway Indians, a peace that would never be broken.

Now it was time for Captain Fleet to speak between the two men—to interpret for them. Not an easy task. Algonquin, which was spoken by the Pascataways, said much in one word while the English used many words for a single thought.

Captain Fleet began, "King of far-off country gave this land to white man." He made a sign with his hands.

Uwanno folded his arms, thinking. He was not pleased.

Captain Fleet went on, "Indians live on land too. White man and Indian all friends. White man wish to settle in territory of Pascataways under protection of Uwanno."

Uwanno thought for some time. He spoke to Kittamaquund and the counselor, trying to understand. Did they dare trust these strange people?

Uwanno looked at Governor Calvert suspiciously. What if he were a demon from across the big water?

Uwanno asked, "Why do you come?"

And Governor Calvert told him, "We come to establish a home for religious freedom in this land, named Maryland for Henrietta Maria, wife of white man's king."

Then one of the priests spoke, "We come to bring the gospel of Jesus Christ to your people, to all who wish to hear."

When Uwanno heard the words of the priest he was moved. He did not understand but he felt a trust behind the words. He was silent for some time in deep thought. After awhile he turned to Kittamaquund and said, "Not long ago I had a dream."

"Tell us the dream."

Uwanno began, "In my dream, two white priests appeared to me. And a voice said, 'These are the men who from their souls love you and all of your tribe, and they bring with them those blessings by which you can be happy if you wish.'"

The Indians muttered together. They all wished for happiness. Kittamaquund wished it for himself and for Little Girl.

"Could it be that these two priests are the ones in my dream?" asked Uwanno.

The Indians nodded. "It is an omen." Mosorcoques and Kittamaquund agreed.

While all this discussion was going on, Governor Calvert was watching the braves on the bank. Better to have them friends than enemies.

After much thought Uwanno said to the governor, "Sit down where you wish, any place in my territory." And Governor Calvert was pleased.

The priests said, "*Dominus vobiscum*—The Lord be with you."

Then Uwanno, Kittamaquund, Mosorcoques and Nicoatucen returned to the shore.

The *Dove* pulled anchor, unfurled sails and, catching a light breeze, went down the creek the way she had come.

The Indians watched. When the *Dove* had gone out of sight Uwanno turned to his people and said, "In three suns we will have a feast to our gods in honor of peace with the white man. We will dance to the fire god, to the sun god, to the god of corn and the god of rain."

"*Dum*, dum, dum, dum. *Dum*, dum, dum, dum." The drummer told the news. The Indians rejoiced. The children shouted and cheered.

Everyone was happy, for they all loved a celebration.

Little Girl didn't hear a thing. The wind had rocked her to sleep in the tree. Her small head rested on the edge of her *teckanagin*. Her soft brown arms hung limp.

Kittamaquund saw her as he passed and his heart was touched. Her mother smiled as she lifted the *teckanagin* gently from the tree and swung it onto her back. The other women smiled saying, "See the pretty one."

The men went through the thicket, one behind the other. The women and children waited, then followed them.

An owl called "whooo" and another answered "whooo." It was time for owls. *Wase'ya*, the light, had gone. *Tci-anung*, the big star, was out.

Little Girl slept soundly.

Chapter 4

THE CELEBRATION

THERE WERE many things to do to get ready for the celebration in Pascataway Village.

While the men went hunting, the women chopped wood and laid a fire just beyond the edge of the wigwams. This was the best time of year for a big fire. It was nearly planting time, and the wood ashes would be fine fertilizer for the corn hills.

Everybody was too busy to keep an eye on the youngest children. Little Girl and Nisha-Nabi, young son of Mosorcoques, were always in the way.

"Lay logs here and here and build a fence," suggested Little Girl's mother. And soon with the logs this way and that, they made a pen.

"In you go, Little Girl."

"In you go, Nisha-Nabi, and you go too, daughter of Nicoatucen."

Some of the big girls gathered shiny stones and colored shells for the small children to play with. Little Girl and her friends played there all day.

At sundown the hunters came home. Kittamaquund brought in a fat turkey hen and two young rabbits.

"Give me turkey feathers," he said to one of his wives. And after she plucked the bird he made a feather ruffle and tied it around his legs, below the knee. Everybody laughed at him as he strutted up and down saying, "*Shag-a-nash*—white man. Governor-man."

Uwanno walked in, arms folded, and said, "A deer lies on the ledge by the locust grove." He wouldn't think of bringing it home. That was women's work.

The best catch was made by Nicoatucen. He killed a bear—a mighty skinny one. "He sleep all winter. He just awake. No locusts and honey yet," Nicoatucen said.

But the others said, "Mmmmmm, bear meat!" Even if it was a thin bear, it was still bear. Everybody was tired of deer and turkey. Nobody had set tooth in a chunk of bear meat for three moons. They could hardly wait.

The next day the women skinned, cleaned and quartered the bear and the deer and dragged them into town on pine branches.

While some of the women scraped the hides to preserve them, Little Girl's mother prepared corn pone and hominy for the feast.

By the time three days had passed everything was ready.

It was a grand occasion for the whole tribe, but especially grand for Little Girl. It was her first big party. Oh, she had been to dances and campfires, riding on her mother's back, but this time she would walk on her own two feet.

The drum sounded. *"Dum,* dum, dum, dum. *Dum,* dum, dum, dum." Time to gather.

The women and children came out of their arched wigwams. They stood to one side waiting for the men to go first.

"The Tayac comes."

"Aaaaa," they said in admiration as Uwanno stepped out of the palace. He was dressed in his royal buckskin cloak, ornamented with shells in circular rows. He had three strings of beads around his neck and a long string of dog's teeth with a large polished jewel in front. His face was stained dark with bark juice and painted blue over the high cheek bones, painted red below his long nose.

"How fierce and bold," the women murmured in approval.

Uwanno folded his arms. He walked through the village with majestic dignity.

Then came Kittamaquund. He was dressed much like his brother, in buckskin cape with his face painted to look like the devil god.

As Kittamaquund turned to follow his brother, Little Girl broke away from her mother and toddled after him, saying "Tu-wee, tu-wee." She was dressed up for the celebration. She wore a string of blue beads around her neck and a small red feather tied to her hair with a slim doeskin thong.

Everybody laughed seeing her.

"Come back, Little Girl, come back," her mother called, but Little Girl kept on. The other women said, "She does not know that a woman must be quiet before men."

Little Girl folded her tiny arms, pulled in her chin and stalked behind her father, stepping high, imitating him.

Everyone shouted with laughter—men, women and

children. Not Kittamaquund. He turned, glowered, saying in anger, "This is a religious ceremony. This is not a time to laugh."

Then he saw his daughter and he too had to laugh. "The gods themselves would laugh at Little Girl," he said as he picked her up and set her on his shoulder, where all could see the small red feather above the crowd.

The procession went along through town to the place where the pile of brush and wood lay ready for the ceremonial fire.

When everybody was assembled, Uwanno placed a live coal from the palace fire on dry leaves under the brush. A flame licked, then caught and leaped into the air. For a few minutes the fire burned brightly.

When the fire settled into a steady burn, the Indians formed two circles around it—the children and young people nearest the fire and the men and women in a larger circle outside. Little Girl's mother carried her now.

Nicoatucen threw deer fat on the fire. The blaze leaped.

Everyone raised his hands to heaven, then raised his voice to heaven, shouting, "*Yaho! Yaho!*" honoring the fire god. "*Yaho! Yaho!*" to the god of corn, of water and of the sun.

Mosorcoques brought a large bag in which was a pipe and powder called *potu.*

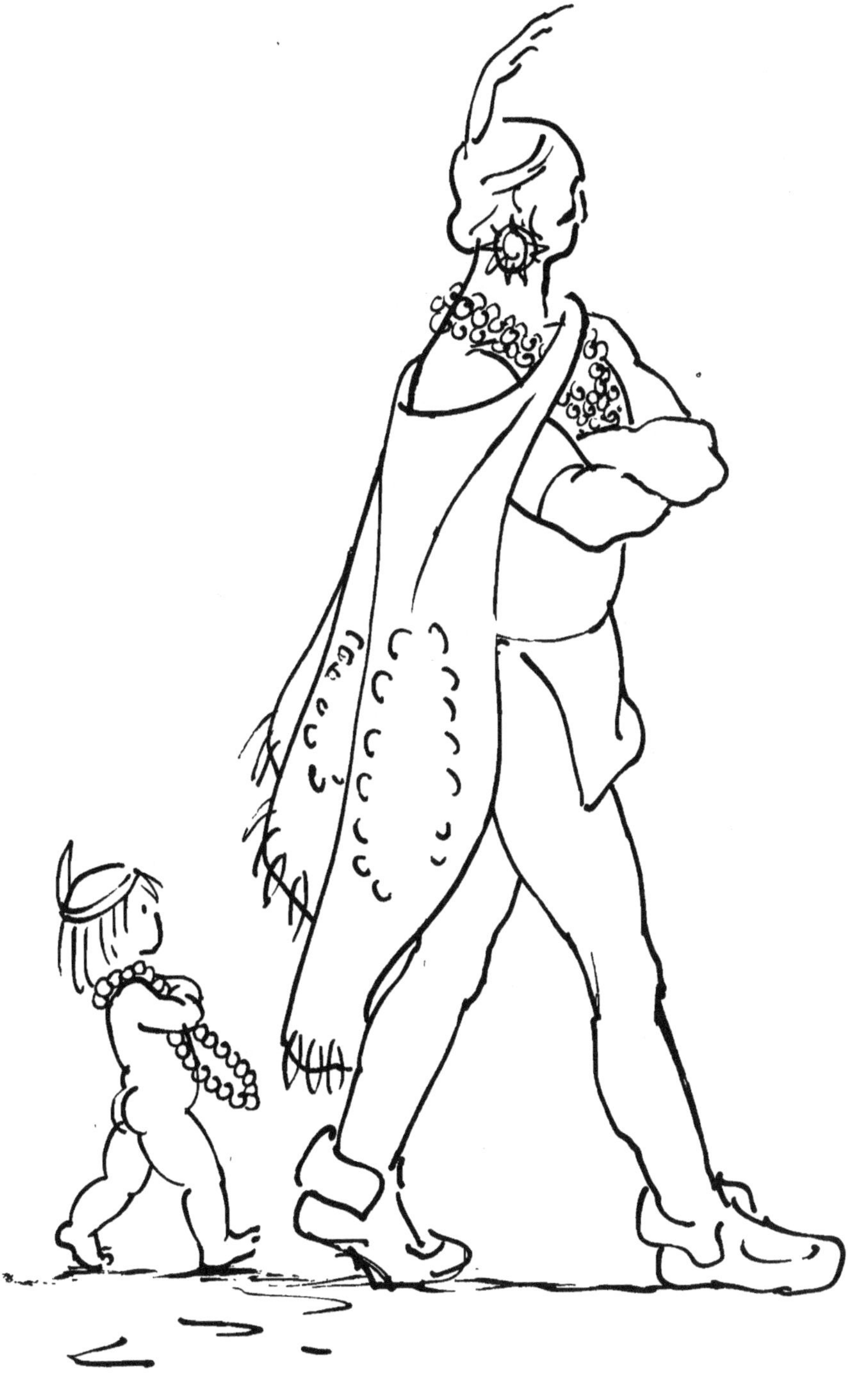

Mosorcoques carried the bag around the fire and the boys and girls followed singing—first the boys, then the girls—"*Yaho! Yaho!*"

Then the bag was opened and the big pipe filled with *potu*. Uwanno lighted the pipe, drew smoke and blew it over his whole body—feet, arms, legs—saying, "I consecrate myself to the service of my god."

Next Kittamaquund smoked the *potu* and consecrated himself with its smoke. The pipe was passed to each and everyone until all had smoked, until all had consecrated themselves to service.

Once again they formed in two lines—the young folks in one and the old folks in the other—and they circled around the dying fire shouting, "*Taho! Taho!*"

At last the celebration was over, and it was time to eat. What a feast!

"Mmmmmm. Bear meat, first of the season. Turkey, pone, hominy. Good!" Everybody ate until his belly was as fat as a possum. Little Girl ate all she could hold and licked her fingers because they tasted so good. Then she rolled over and went to sleep like a pup. This had been the biggest day of her life, but there were bigger days to come, lots of them.

Chapter 5

Little Princess

URING the next few years Little Girl grew from a charming, fat, brown baby into a smart and beautiful little girl. She learned to say, *pe-na-sheè-enss*, little bird. To say, *Shag-a-nash*, meaning white man, and *Anishee-nabie*, Indian. She learned the way of the for- est and the animals that lived there. She learned the way of the wide sky and the birds. She learned the way of the creek and the fish swimming in it, and the plants in its clear waters.

She learned to play with the other children, to race and to win. She learned to help her mother, to weave, to mold clay, to care for the younger children. She grew gentle and well-mannered and modest as she grew tall. But sometime within those few years something took place to change her whole life.

Kittamaquund wanted to wear the royal cloak trimmed with shells set in circles. He wanted to wear the collar with the great stone. He wanted his daughter to be the princess. So he slew his brother—or rumor said he did.

Shhhhh. Best not speak of it. No one saw. There was no proof. Perhaps it was a bear that killed the Emperor.

Those were cruel times. The savages, used to violence, were not shocked at the rumor.

Uwanno was dead. That only was certain.

"Now Kittamaquund is Tayac," the people said. "Now Kittamaquund is emperor of the Pascataways and many other tribes."

They hailed Little Girl as Princess, Neen-daniss-enss-Kittamaquund, daughter of Kittamaquund.

Little Princess felt almost the same as she did when she was called Little Girl. She would run faster now, jump higher perhaps.

Kittamaquund ruled his tribe wisely, but he was troubled. He sacrificed his first deer, his first fish, to Okee. He danced in honor of his god. Surely Okee would not be angry with him. Still he was full of fear. He knew no peace except in his love for his daughter, Little Princess.

When Kittamaquund was not making decisions for the tribe, or judging his people, or fishing or hunting— for even a ruler must hunt to live—he spent his time with his daughter.

He taught her to be silent and let the wind speak.

He taught her to think clearly before she spoke. And best of all, he played games with her.

One day, the day that Little Princess was five years old, the two of them took their favorite walk through the thicket of trees to the bluff overlooking the creek.

They were a handsome pair. Kittamaquund tall, strong and straight as an arrow; Little Princess up to his elbow.

Kittamaquund was silent as he walked with great strides but the princess was as gay as a lark. She danced along, hanging on his arm. It wasn't easy to keep up with him but it was fun trying. She was carrying her birthday present, a new shuttlecock made of a sassafras knuckle and turkey feathers, and two smooth wooden bats.

"Today I made a bowl all by myself," she boasted.

"And yesterday I skinned a squirrel." She looked up at her father and skipped twice, hoping he'd be pleased. He did not say a word.

"Soon, Mother is going to teach me to cook a beaver stew the way you like it. And pone too. Already I grind corn as well as Mother does. She told me so."

Still Kittamaquund was silent.

They came out on the bluff.

"Look, look! *Oo-nish-she-shin*," she said pointing to a pair of blue herons wading in the shallow water.

She laughed gaily. "Old stick-legs! See them pick their way on stilts." She imitated the herons walking.

Still Kittamaquund did not laugh. He was silent.

Little Princess took his hand, looked up at him, saying, "You are not pleased with me."

He spoke slowly. "I am pleased. I want more for you, much more."

Little Princess tugged at his hand and said, "And I want much more from you. Take this paddle and play with me. Catch. I'll beat you."

She ran off a way and whacked the shuttlecock high into the air. "Don't let it fall. Oh, get it, Father, quick."

Whack! Up it went again. "Whee, see it fly. Look out. There she goes!"

What fun they had! And it was a tight match. Kittamaquund was strong and sure. Little Princess was as quick as a hummingbird as she dashed in, out, and around.

They played until they were tired. Then they sat on the edge of the bluff with their feet hanging over and watched the sun go down.

Everything was beautiful and still. The forest on the other side of the creek made deep blue shadows on the water. The trees in the forest behind them rustled and whispered to one another as the wind passed.

"There is a crane." The big bird flew right over their heads, so low they could see his pink feet.

Little Princess and Kittamaquund sat close together in peace until the herons and the cranes went to bed, and the swallows began to circle in the sky.

When the first owl hooted, Kittamaquund said, "Little Princess, I have no sister. My brother is gone. The law says the rule must return to another child of a daughter of our founder. But I will change the law. I am the ruler. When I am gone I want *you* to rule our people. I want you to be the *Queen*."

"*Me* Queen! *Me* rule!" She jumped to her feet.

She puffed out her little chest and gave a hearty laugh. Then she started to run, shouting, "Who can catch the Queen? Who can catch the Queen?"

She raced through the thicket like a fawn, her tough bare feet hardly touching the pine needles, her black hair flying.

Kittamaquund smiled as he followed her home in the dusk.

She was still very young. There was plenty of time.

Chapter 6

A Visitor

THE FOLLOWING summer Little Princess was playing on the bluff again. This time she was playing with the son of Mosorcoques the counselor, the son of Nicoatucen, and several of the other children.

They were pretending to be hunters in the territory of the enemy. Each child held a small bow made like a real one with feathers on the tip and an arrow with a sharpened stone for a point.

"I will be the look-out scout," said Mosorcoques' son. The Princess said, "No, it's my turn. You were scout last time."

"But you are only a girl!"

Little Princess stamped her foot and repeated, "It's my turn, even if I am a girl." So the boys gave in.

Little Princess ran down the bank as stealthily as a fox, without a sound. She crept through the bushes, looking this way and that. Now she was right at the water's edge. How cool it looked! And she was hot and sticky from playing hard.

She laid her bow and arrow on the bank and slid into the water like a beaver. She swam out a way, her long hair floating behind her. All at once she spied a strange man walking along the bank. He was tall, dressed in black and oh, oh, did he have horns? She dared not look again. Quickly she turned around, swam back and scrambled ashore. She shook herself like a fox as she ran up the bank shouting, "A demon is after me! A black demon with horns. Run, run!"

"Run, run!" the other children shouted, and they ran for home with Little Princess out in front.

Little Princess' mother was grinding corn with a stone pestle just outside the palace door. Kittamaquund was there too, putting an edge on his axe.

"A demon is coming," shouted the Princess. "Tall and black with horns. Run, run and hide!"

"Softly, speak softly," her mother said, "or you will attract him."

Kittamaquund laid aside his soapstone, saying calmly, "Are you sure about the horns? Nicoatucen has told me a white man's priest is coming. His canoe went down. He walks on foot to our village."

"*Shag-a-nash!*" exclaimed Mosorcoques' son.

"*Shag-a-nash*," Little Princess said, her eyes wide with excitement, for a white man was almost as exciting as a demon.

"*Shag-a-nash*," repeated the other children and they ran off to tell the news.

"Be sure of what your eye sees before you speak," Little Princess' father told her. "Come, let us go to meet the white man."

Kittamaquund started for the thicket but Little Princess ducked into the palace saying, "Wait, wait for me." And a moment later she returned with her blue beads around her neck.

"I hope the white man will think my beads are pretty," she said as she and Kittamaquund started down the well-worn path.

Before they had reached the third tall pine tree they met the stranger coming toward them in his long black robe with a large leather-covered Bible in his arms.

"*Quay-quay*," Kittamaquund greeted him.

"*Quay-quay*," said the priest holding out his hand. "I am Father Andrew White from St. Mary's."

Little Princess looked out from behind her father. There were no horns at all. Feeling ashamed of herself, she ran to the priest, took his hand in her small copper hands and looking up at him said, "I am Little Princess. See my blue beads?"

Father White smiled at her. "You swim fast and run fast, Little Princess."

"You saw me?"

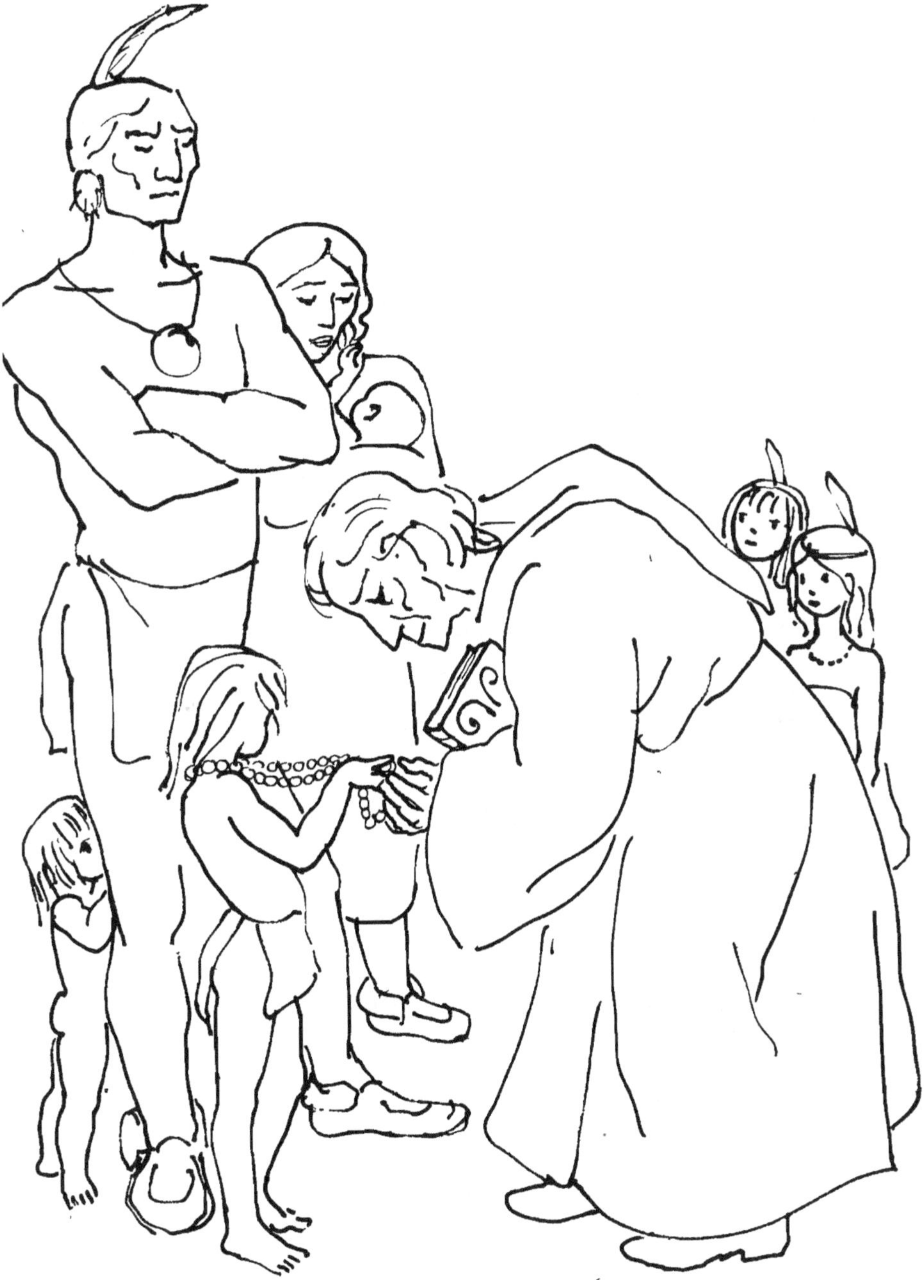

Father White nodded. He saw the child's bright eyes and the father's pride in her. Father White was interested in everything, every person and every animal that came his way. He stooped and examined the blue beads.

"They are beautiful, Little Princess. Very beautiful. They came from the other side of the ocean from a country called Italy." He spoke slowly in Algonquin.

"It-a-ly, It-a-ly," said Little Princess.

Father White explained, "From Italy to Spain, across the ocean to Barbados."

"And I bought them for my daughter at the Kent Island trading post for fifty beaver skins," Kittamaquund told him.

Little Princess ran on ahead to spread the news that the priest was coming. "It-a-ly," she repeated. She liked the sound of the new word.

"*Shag-a-nash* says my blue beads were made in It-a-ly," she shouted as she ran into the palace.

"Speak softly, child," her mother said and shook her head, for at times Little Princess was much too noisy for a well-reared Indian girl.

The minute Father White came into the palace his strong personality drew everyone to him.

"Stay with us," said Kittamaquund. "Make the palace your home."

"God bless you," said Father White.

"And me too?" asked Little Princess.

Father White laughed, "Yes, you too, and all of your people."

"Sleep in my bed," Kittamaquund offered.

Father White said no, he would sleep on a mat outside Kittamaquund's door.

"Sleep on my mat," said Little Princess.

Father White was grateful for the warm welcome. Perhaps losing his supplies and his boat was a blessing after all.

That evening the whole village had supper together out under the trees. The emperor's wife, anxious to please the visitor, made a fish stew and served it to him herself. One of Kittamaquund's wives made corn pone, crisp and tasty. Another wife offered the priest wineberries, oily, red and tart.

After supper the men of the tribe sat in a circle under the trees and smoked their pipes. The women and children sat on the ground close by and waited for one of the braves to speak. There was a long silence.

Finally Mosorcoques stood up and with arms folded told how Nanabozho, the man-being, the hero-man, came down to earth from the cloud country. How he helped man to do all things. How he sometimes made mistakes, did tricks, told false stories, to make himself faulty like man. He told a story of the time when all the tribes were hungry. He told how the man-being sent Mondawmin down to earth. How Mondawmin died and was buried in the ground. How he came up green and grew into corn to feed the people.

Then the men turned to Father White, waiting for him to speak.

Father White looked at the circle of dark faces around him. He was deeply moved. This was the moment he had waited for, planned and worked for. He thought back to the years he had spent as a priest in England—prison, banishment, long days and nights of study. He remembered his missionary work and his years of teaching as a Jesuit priest and his work teaching in Spain. He remembered his dream of working in America, and here he was at last.

How to begin? He prayed for the answer. And the answer came, "Begin at the beginning."

He opened his Bible at the first page and began to read in Algonquin. "In the beginning, God created the heaven and the earth. And the earth was without form and void; and darkness was upon the face of the deep. And the spirit of God moved upon the waters."

The men nodded. Little Princess crept inside the circle of men and sat down close to Father White. The other children followed and no one called them back.

Father White went on, "And God said Let there be

light," and he read on and on the wonderful story of creation.

When the sun went down and he could no longer see to read, he closed the Book and talked on and on. The moon came up and a gentle breeze blew in from the creek, making a soft whisper in the pines overhead. A whippoorwill called and called. A fox barked his hollow bark and the dogs stood up and bayed.

The Indians listened in wonder when he told how God collected the water into seas. How He made man from dust and woman from man.

Tci-anung, the big star, came out.

The moon sailed higher and higher. It was time for sleep.

Chapter 7

KITTAMAQUUND AND THE EVIL SPIRIT

WHEN NEXT THE SUN went down, Father White told the story of the Flood. At the end Kittamaquund said, "God punished the people for their wicked ways, like our god, Okee. He punishes us. He sends famine, sickness and death."

"God forgives those who are sorry," Father White said gently, and he told them about Jesus and the love of God.

For some time Kittamaquund thought about all that Father White had said. His god did not forgive. Kittamaquund wanted to know more about Jesus but "A wise man steps slowly in matters of good and evil," he said to himself. There was no hurry.

The next night when Father White told the Christmas story, they loved it and wanted more. But Father White wisely asked one of them to tell him a story.

So the next evening Mosorcoques told about the fire god and what wonderful things he did for man.

And another time Nicoatucen told the story of a famous bear hunt. The children, outside the circle of men, listened wide-eyed. But when the story ended with the big bear dead and the hunter proud and haughty, Little Princess whispered to Mosorcoques' son, "That is not as good a story as Jesus," and the rest of the children agreed.

Father White told all of the grand stories—the Good Samaritan, the great draught of fishes, the Prodigal Son, the feeding of the multitude—one by one. The Indians understood for they were simple people too, like fishermen and carpenters. They understood love.

Whenever the hunters came home and the women were through work for the day and the children were tired out from playing, Father White would talk to them and answer their questions.

Slowly they began to know Jesus. But they hung back.

"Okee will be angry with us if we turn to this Jesus," they said in fear.

Father White was not discouraged. The Gospel was two thousand years old. If only he could win over the emperor, the rest of the tribe would follow him.

Then one night when they were all gathered together, Kittamaquund stood up, folded his arms and said, "Now I will tell a true story. Last night I had a dream."

Everyone listened eagerly, for they believed in dreams.

Kittamaquund went on, "In my dream, my own father, long dead, appeared to me and with him was a god of dim color. The dim god begged me not to forsake him."

There was a long pause. Little Princess wished her father would continue. She was anxious to learn what happened next, but she dared not speak out.

Finally Kittamaquund went on, "Governor Calvert and Father White appeared with a god, radiant, marvelous. The god beckoned gently and then the dream faded. What does it mean?"

There were murmurs among the men as each interpreted the dream.

Mosorcoques and the medicine men thought perhaps Okee was angry because Father White was there with them. They advised Kittamaquund to hold a feast and make sacrifices for Okee.

Father White said perhaps the god in the dream was Jesus Himself.

Perhaps.

Anyway, after the dream Kittamaquund listened to Father White attentively and asked many questions. When Father White taught the Princess to say "The Lord is my shepherd, I shall not want" in English, Kittamaquund was pleased and said, "She must learn to speak the white man's language. Some day she must speak like you and the white Governor." And because Kittamaquund was so pleased he said to Father White, "I will worship your Jesus, too, along with our gods."

But Father White said, "No. One God, only one. A God of love, not fear."

Kittamaquund shook his head. One God was not enough for all of his sins.

Then one day he fell ill. The medicine men were called. They came dressed in costumes wild enough to scare the devil himself—feathers around their waists, horns on their heads, more feathers around their ankles, streaks of paint, white, blue and red, on face, arms and back. They danced around Kittamaquund's bed, they shouted and beat the drum to drive away the evil spirits. They believed that an evil spirit entered a man's body and made him ill.

Kittamaquund did not get better. His fever went higher and no wonder with all that racket. The next morning he was very ill indeed. The Indian priests came and gave sacrifices to their god. They called to him loudly, they shouted, but he did not hear. By night it was feared that the emperor might die.

Little Princess was full of sorrow. It was terrible to see her mighty father full of an evil spirit.

She begged Father White to chase the demon out.

The good priest was uneasy. Suppose the Emperor should die? Much of his work would be lost. Still, he must try.

He sent the others out of the palace. Alone and in quiet he prayed beside the sick man. He anointed him with holy water and he bled him, as was the custom in those days.

Something worked—prayer, faith, or the bleeding? Father White himself did not know which but he was grateful. "*Deo Gratias*, Thanks be to God," he said.

By morning Kittamaquund was feeling better. He sat up and called out to Father White, "Your God has saved me. I want to be a Christian at once."

Again Father White said, "*Deo Gratias*."

"Baptize me. I want to be a Christian. Baptize me now." Kittamaquund was impatient.

"And me too," said Little Princess who was listening to every word.

Kittamaquund said, "No, no. Not you, Princess. Not yet. While I lay sick unto death and was afraid I might leave you, I made plans. You must learn all that the white man knows, how he speaks, how he reads the words in his book. Then you may become a Christian."

Father White thought it best to wait for Little Princess, as the father wished.

Father White had plans himself. He wanted everyone to see the Emperor baptized so others would hear
of it and follow him.

"Let us send for Governor Calvert and his friends in
St. Mary's. We will build a chapel here and have a celebration for all to witness."

Kittamaquuund did not want to wait. After awhile
he said, "If I wait could I wear the clothes like Governor
Calvert's?"

Father White nodded, "Yes."

"I wait. But how long?"

"Three days to spread the news, three days to get
ready, four days to get here, one day's grace," said
Father White.

So the day was set for the baptism of Kittamaquuund,
the Tayac, Emperor of the Pascataways, ruler of the
Potopacoe, the Yaocomicoe, the Chopticoe, and all the
other tribes in that territory; with the exception of the
Anacostan.

Chapter 8

A Baptism and a Wedding

*N*ICOATUCEN paddled fast to St. Mary's with the invitation to the baptism. Scouts that he met along the Potomac carried the news from tribe to tribe. Soon the whole of Maryland had heard of the Tayac's conversion.

Back in Pascataway Village some of the braves helped Father White build a chapel for the occasion—a sapling chapel covered with bark. They helped him build a wooden altar and a cross of wood from the dogwood tree.

Kittamaquund stood around, getting in the way. He was too excited to be of use to anyone.

"My wives will be Christians too," he told Father White. And when the priest said, "A Christian has only *one* wife," Kittamaquund was distressed.

"Only *one* wife? But *I* have three already and they are all fine women."

"Only *one*," repeated Father White. "One God. One wife."

This was a blow. Kittamaquund went off into the woods alone and sat under a tall oak to think it over.

He recalled his marriages. How each wife had brought him a fine beaver stew and how he had given her a beaver skin in return, showing that he accepted her as his wife.

Choose one of the three? How could he? Each was pleasant, hard-working, young, and two of them had children.

Children? What of Little Princess? He jumped to his feet. There was no question. Little Princess' mother was his choice. The other two wives would have to go. He could not part with Little Princess.

Kittamaquund went straight into the palace and told the wives of his decision and he went right outdoors again before they could speak a word.

Lucky for him that he didn't hear their comments. For even Little Princess' mother was angry.

"He keeps me because of the child," she said, "not because I am his favorite wife."

That made the other wives feel a little better.

The next day the two wives moved out of the palace. Not far—just next door—and Kittamaquund helped them move.

"I will find a good husband for each of you soon," he told them. The women were pleased to hear that. And they were not too upset anyway, for they knew that they would be cared for. They knew they would not be lonely or neglected. Whenever the tribe had food they would eat. There would always be a wigwam and a mat for them.

The incident was forgotten quickly for there was so much work to do that everyone had to help.

At last, when the work was all finished, the day of the baptism arrived. Quite early—the sun was still below the treetops—a scout ran out of the forest and said, "Three canoes are coming."

Little Princess and the rest of the children ran fast through the thicket, scaring up two rabbits in their path. And a squirrel in a pine tree scolded and scolded as they ran out onto the bluff.

"There, see?" shouted Little Princess pointing below. The children lined up and watched the canoes nose into the bank. They watched the visitors from Potopaco Village step ashore.

"Don't let them see us," said Little Princess suddenly shy and wild as a fawn.

The children dropped flat on the ground and kept perfectly still until the strangers had gone on through the thicket. Then they jumped, laughing heartily, ran down the bank and jumped into the creek. They scrubbed themselves with sand, laughing and splashing each other for fun. Once the bath was over they climbed up the bank and ran around and around in circles to dry off. Then off for home where they greased themselves all over with bear grease to keep off the mosquitoes.

Little Princess was combing her hair with a chip when someone shouted outside, "Another canoe is coming!"

"Hurry, let's see it." And the children ran back to the bluff in time to see the big log canoe arrive from St. Mary's.

"*Shag-a-nash. Shag-a-nash,*" the children shouted when they saw the white people. Then, pretending to be scared of them, they ran off into the woods without waiting to take a second look. They played out of sight under the trees until they heard the drum.

"*Dum*, dum, dum, dum. *Dum*, dum, dum, dum," telling that it was time for the baptism.

God set the stage with one of His most perfect days— bright blue sky with white clouds, a gentle breeze blowing inland from the creek.

Birds sang in the trees and Father White was sure that angels sang in heaven.

The people from St. Mary's and the other guests went into the chapel. The children came in silently and sat on a log off to one side where they could see everything.

"There is Governor Calvert," someone said aloud, and pointed to him.

The Princess watched Governor Calvert and the women with him. She had never seen white women before. Little Princess wished she had a dress like theirs with a full skirt of fancy material. She wished she had a blouse with long sleeves trimmed with lace and a little hat on top of her head with a point down low on her forehead.

"Who are the *shag-a-nash-equay* (the white women) next to Governor Calvert?" she asked in a whisper. "What are their names?"

"Mistress Margaret Brent," Nicoatucen told her, "and her sister Mary."

"They are looking at us, see?" Little Princess said, ducking behind Nicoatucen. "And see the man with them? He's looking this way. His face is pale as the moon and his hair is as light as a rabbit."

"Giles Brent, brother of Mistress Margaret and Mistress Mary. The Brents own much land and tobacco." Nicoatucen looked up and said, "There is Father White. Sh-sh! It's time for the service to begin."

"There's Kittamaquund!"

Kittamaquund, dressed at last in a soft white shirt with ruffled collar, came in and knelt before the wooden altar. Several others knelt beside him.

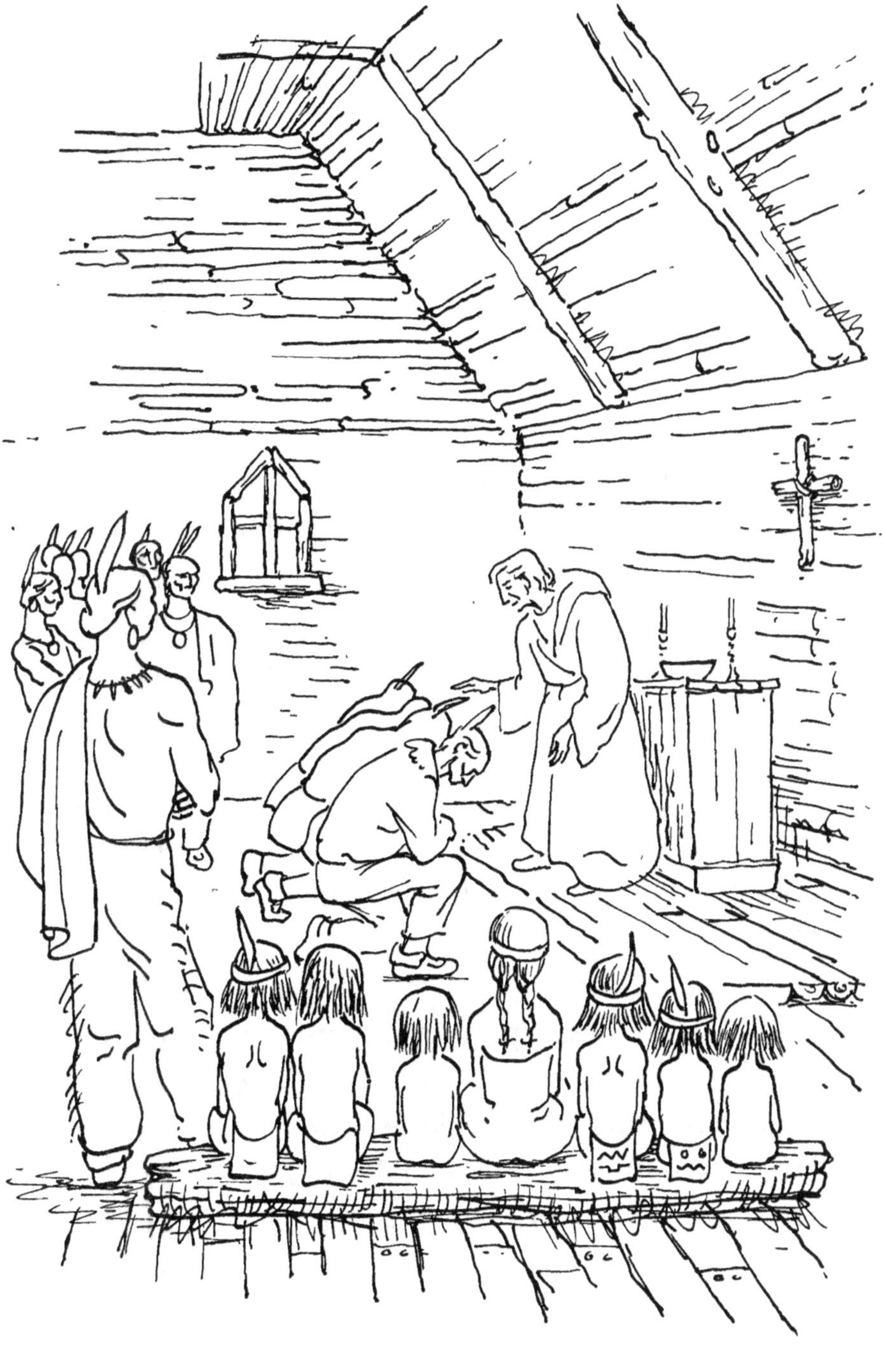

After a long silence—not even a cricket chirped outside the window—Father White spoke strange words in a low voice.

Little Princess did not understand at all but the sound of prayer made a tingle run down her spine.

Father White blessed water from the creek and Little Princess felt that it was indeed made into sacred water. She watched the priest place water on her father's brow, and by a solemn mystery he became a Christian.

One by one the others were made Christians. And everyone who became a Catholic that day was given a Christian name.

The Queen was to be called Mary. An infant was called Ann. Mosorcoques became John and his son Robert.

Kittamaquund was given the name of Charles.

"I want to be called Leonard after Governor Calvert," he said, but Father White told him that Charles was the name of the great king of England and that was better still.

At last the ceremony was over. Kittamaquund, radiant inside and out, said proudly, "Now I am Charles, the Christian." When everybody told him he looked like the Governor in his fancy clothes, his chest swelled out with pride until he nearly burst his ruffled shirt.

But Little Princess frowned, saying to him, "You and

my mother are Christians and have new names while I am still me."

"Be patient, your turn will come," her father said.

Little Princess did not want to be patient. That was no fun.

Later when the sun was directly overhead, she ate roast turkey and fresh baked pone with the visitors. English was spoken—first the Governor, then Giles Brent, then one of the women. Not being able to understand a single word of it, Little Princess frowned, ripped the meat off a turkey bone and chewed angrily with her strong white teeth. They did not know how to speak Algonquin and she did.

After lunch there was a wedding. Although Little Princess' father and mother had already been married Indian fashion, they were married again by Father White in the chapel before all of the people.

"Do you, Charles, take this woman to be your lawful wedded wife?" And the Emperor, dressed in his rumpled, ruffled shirt, said, "Yes."

A baptism, a feast and a wedding all in one day.

The next day the guests left for their homes. Father White went along with them back to St. Mary's, for he was very tired and needed a long rest. His work was completed at Pascataway Village. The Emperor was a Christian. Now others would follow in his footsteps.

Little Princess hated to say good-by to Father White. She would miss him and his wonderful stories about Jesus.

"Let's play white man," she said as soon as the last canoe went from sight around the bend in the creek.

And for weeks the children made up new words that sounded like English words and some that sounded like Latin. Little Princess wore a whole deerskin tied around her waist. "*Shag-a-nash-equay*," she said, switching her skirt, pretending to be Mistress Brent.

Kittamaquund watched the children playing. His daughter was growing up. He wanted her to learn to speak English like the white women. He wanted her to learn to read the Bible like Father White, to become a Christian like her father.

He would take her to St. Mary's to study. Perhaps some day she would not have to pretend.

Chapter 9

THE TRIP TO ST. MARY'S

THE WEATHER turned hot and dry. There was no rain at all. Springs were low. Corn dried up. Green leaves turned brown.

Deer, rabbits and squirrels traveled north searching for food.

The Indians grew lean and hungry.

"Famine." They spoke the dreaded word in fear.

They prayed to the rain god. They danced to him and gave sacrifices of fish and precious corn, but it did not rain.

Charles Kittamaquund, the Christian, prayed for rain too.

No rain came but his prayer was answered. Father White sent another priest to Pascataway Village with enough corn to keep the tribe alive until spring.

Charles Kittamaquund gave thanks to God, and so did his people.

Weeks passed. Then one day there was the familiar "Hawn, hawn, hawn" overhead.

"Wild geese, Father," shouted Little Princess, pointing to the sky.

"Winter is coming. The geese fly south."

Later on the snow fell soft in the night. The children hauled out a buffalo hide and slid down the hill on it, but there wasn't enough snow.

"Next time it will snow more," they said.

And they were right. It wasn't long before it snowed and snowed. Deep, white and still.

Snow was just as good as rain. The springs filled up again. The creek froze over.

Kittamaquund spent much time with Mosorcoques, the counselor.

"Little Princess is to rule after me," he said.

Mosorcoques was doubtful. "The tribe will elect Weghucasso, for he is next in line."

Kittamaquund said, "*I* am the Emperor. *I* will change the laws. Little Princess is to be Queen after me."

Mosorcoques listened, but did not speak.

Kittamaquund called his daughter to him and said, "When the ice melts on the creek I will take you to St. Mary's. It is time for you to study."

"Yes," said Little Princess, "it's time to go," and she ran all over the village to tell the news.

What fun it would be! Her first long trip away from

home. Away from home? That was an awful thought. Maybe she didn't want to go after all.

"I will miss my home. I believe I will not go."

Kittamaquund frowned, "You will go. You will learn English. You will become a Christian, and then you may return home."

"Yes, Father."

The snows melted and the ice melted. It was time to go.

"Tomorrow we leave."

Everybody in the village was up at dawn. The people trailed through the thicket and gathered on the bluff to bid the travelers good-by.

Little Princess was in high spirits and she looked a princess from tip to toe. Now that she was seven years old, she wore a doeskin shirt with a decoration of beads on the front and a skirt of soft leather with a border of beads and a fringe. She wore leggings, too, and a cloak to keep out the cold. A cloak, soft and warm made of deerskin, ankle length, with feathers woven in the border to match her new moccasins. She carried her doll and a beaded bag full of treasures—a smooth white stone, two head bands, a red feather, a dog's tooth, a rabbit's tail, and her string of blue beads.

Two canoes were going to St. Mary's.

Little Princess took her place in the middle of Kitta-maquund's canoe with the blanket rolls, the clothes and the bows and arrows.

It was a fine, strong canoe, more than six arm-lengths from bow to stern. Kittamaquund had made it himself the year he became a man. With his father, he had found the gum tree in the forest—a tall, strong, healthy tree. He had cut the tree down with his own axe. He had stripped off the bark and cut the log. He had soaked the log all winter long and then dried it in the sun. He had hollowed the log with red-hot stones, burned out the center until it was a light shell and shaped the bow and stern until it was in perfect balance. His paddles were balanced, too, and strong. For years the canoe had served him well.

Now, standing beside it, Kittamaquund, the Emperor, raised his hand to his people and said, "Mosorcoques will take my place as your ruler until I return."

Then he and Nicoatucen pushed the canoe out into the water. They took their places, Kittamaquund in the stern, Nicoatucen in the bow.

They dipped paddles and the canoe shot forward.

"Good-by. Good-by." Half joy, half sorrow. Little Princess hugged her doll close and did not look back.

The other canoe followed close behind. Loaded with beaver skins for trading, it sat low in the water. Two

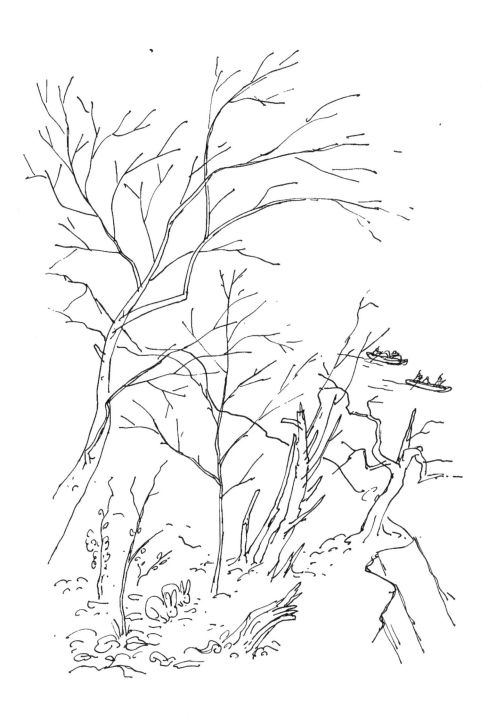

strong warriors riding in it kept a sharp look-out as they paddled along.

"How far is it to St. Mary's, Father?"

"Down where the river flows into the great bay."

"How long will it take us to go there?"

"Three more times the sun will rise and set, if our paddles dip swiftly."

"A long, long way."

Little Princess settled back snug and warm, her doll cradled in her cape.

"Look there," she pointed to a tall bare tree which was on the verge of falling into the water. "See, there is a big old eagle. He's watching us."

And further along they saw two men fishing. They waved and the men waved back.

The sun rose higher and the gentle motion of the canoe lulled Little Princess to sleep for a short nap. She woke up quickly when Kittamaquund called out, "Big fish. See."

Before the sun was directly overhead the canoe swung left.

"Now we are going into the Potomac River," said Nicoatucen proudly.

"It is like the creek only wider," said Little Princess.

Kittamaquund and Nicoatucen paddled swiftly, expertly—dip, pull, dip, pull.

The river was beautiful, clean, and blue with firm land on either side. Fine groves of trees grew all the way down to the water's edge. As the sun went down, the trees sent dark shadows on the water. A cool breeze began to blow. Swallows swooped in circles across the wide sky.

At night the travelers camped on a beach at a point of land near a bend in the river. Crow's-foot grew all around, showing that a spring was near.

Little Princess was so tired from her first long day of travel that she fell asleep at supper.

The next day the travelers were up with the sun and on their way.

And before the sun went down again they stopped at Potopacoe Village on the east bank of the river in a protected valley. The Potopacoe people were glad to see them and the women cooked fish in a special way, with chestnuts. It was good. Little Princess ate and ate and smacked her lips for more.

In the evening they all sat around and sang songs while one of the braves played on a cittern, a sort of guitar.

When the children went to bed, Kittamaquund sat late talking with the men of the tribe.

The Potopacoe Indians were expert coppersmiths. Kittamaquund bought a bowl and a water pitcher for two arms lengths of *wampumpeak*, the shell used as money.

"A present for Mistress Margaret Brent and Governor Calvert."

At daybreak they were on their way again. The sky was overcast and later a drizzle started that lasted all day. Little Princess didn't mind, for not a drop of water went through her new cloak.

That night they camped on the east bank near St. Clements, beyond the wide mouth of the Wicomico River.

While the men fished and made a fire for supper, Little Princess ran around to stretch her legs. She ran too far. When she turned to go back she did not know which way to go, for all of the trees looked alike.

Was it that way by the oak? No. Was it this way between the pines? Not that way either.

A chill went over the little girl. She was scared.

"Aya," she called and listened for an answer. Again "Aya, aya."

She ran this way and that and she called again. It was almost dark. Suppose—?

All of a sudden a limb snapped under her feet and some animal jumped up quickly and was off in the shadows before she could see what it was.

Now Little Princess really did yell "Aya," and how glad she was to hear her father shout "Aya" beyond the trees!

She ran fast to him, and in no time she was safe by the fire.

"A bear, a fox, or something, almost ate me," she exclaimed, her eyes as big as an owl's.

The men laughed at her saying, "A rabbit, perhaps."

But they did not laugh the next morning when they found bear tracks not far from their campfire.

After a good breakfast of fried fish they were ready to travel again. When the sun was high Little Princess asked, "Aren't we almost there?"

"Almost."

The river grew wider and wider until it was so wide you could hardly see the thin line of trees on the far side.

"The Chesapeake Bay lies beyond," Nicoatucen said. Kittamaquund held his paddle firm to guide the canoe around the bend.

"We are going up St. George's River now. St. Mary's lies on ahead."

Little Princess sat up straight. She could hardly wait to get there. Four long days! She felt as if she'd traveled to the moon and back.

At sundown they paddled past a slender point of

land, on past another point, and into a quiet, crescent cove with the second canoe not far behind.

The canoes nosed into the sandy shore and stopped. St. Mary's at last!

Chapter 10

St. Mary's

THERE is Father White coming to meet us," Little Princess said.

No, it was Father Fisher, priest of St. Mary's.

"*Quay-quay*," Kittamaquund said in greeting, as he stepped ashore.

"*Quay-quay*."

Little Princess frowned. She was disappointed not to see Father White. But when the young priest took her bag of treasures, her doll, gave her his hand and said in halting Algonquin, "I will take you to your friends," she smiled at him brightly and jumped onto the sandy beach.

While Kittamaquund spoke to Nicoatucen about the business of trading the beaver skins, Little Princess looked around. Back from the shore there was a long, low palisade of sharply hewn logs overlooking the water.

"St. Mary's Fort," Father Fisher told her.

Little Princess had heard about the fort. There were the four heavy iron cannons aimed out over the water. She had never seen a cannon before but she'd heard about the white man's gunpowder with its great noise that killed. Surely no enemy would ever take St. Mary's.

Father Fisher led the way up the gentle slope, through scrub pines that grew along a little stream.

Beyond lay a wide field and on one side was the biggest wigwam Little Princess had ever seen.

"Governor Calvert's wigwam," Father Fisher explained.

"Oh, look, *mistatem*—big dogs," Little Princess shouted, seeing horses in the field.

"Governor Calvert's horses from England," the priest told her.

She had heard about big dogs. She had heard how men rode on their backs, but she had never seen one before. She ran over to the fence and climbed up to watch them grazing.

One horse stopped cropping grass and looked at Little Princess with his ears pointed.

"*Quay-quay*, Big Dog," she called to him.

Big Dog whinnied and walked toward her. He was shiny brown with a white spot shaped like an oak leaf on his face.

Little Princess rubbed his nose. She would like to have stayed there talking to him but Father Fisher and Kittamaquund had gone on. She ran to catch up with them.

"I wish Big Dog were mine," she told her father as they walked along Mattaponi Road, the Indian trail that led to Mattaponi Village on the Patuxent River. Kittamaquund did not reply.

After awhile Little Princess said, "If I had Big Dog I would ride and feed him and everything."

Her father smiled. "You like Big Dog?" And Little Princess swinging on his hand said, "Yes, yes."

When they reached the brick chapel of St. Mary's where Main Road branched off and went through beautiful green woods, they took a narrow foot-path across a field.

Little Princess looked all around. It was a lovely place on high ground. She could see small houses with red roofs and chimneys dotted here and there, and several Indian houses like those at home.

Close by there was a large house set among big trees.

"White House, home of Giles Brent," Father Fisher told them.

Little Princess nodded. She guessed "Home" meant wigwam and she remembered Giles Brent, the tall man with fair hair.

They kept on along the path to the adjoining town house, Little Princess taking two steps to Father Fisher's one long stride. A hop-toad jumped out of the way. There was a redbird in the tree.

"Sister's Freehold, home of Mistress Margaret Brent," Father Fisher said as he turned off the path. Little Princess remembered Mistress Margaret Brent and her sister, Mary, too.

Sister's Freehold was a lovely place overlooking the

river. It was a large house almost hidden by a grove of handsome oak trees.

As they crossed the grass the door of Sister's Freehold opened and there was Mistress Margaret Brent, Mistress Mary Brent, brother Giles, and Governor Calvert. And best of all, Father White.

Little Princess ran to him. "*Oo-nish-she-shin! Oo-nish-she-shin!*" she said again and again. "Pretty. Pretty."

"Surely an old man is not pretty," Father White said in Algonquin, "but you are *oo-nish-she-shin equay-enss*—pretty little girl."

"Come in, come in," said Mistress Brent. A funny English word, "come in."

Little Princess held back, wishing she were home. She did not want to "come in." Suddenly she was frightened.

Kittamaquund said sternly, "Stand straight. You are my daughter."

She stood straight and followed her father through the door into a big square room, not pretty and oval like home. An open fire burned brightly in the fireplace at the far end of the room, not in the middle like at home.

Above the fire, candles were burning in tall candlesticks. There was a rug on the floor, as soft as moss, with a big ice-smooth table on it. And there was Father White's Bible!

While the grown people were talking together by the fire, Little Princess opened the Bible and looked inside. Those strange black marks! Could they really tell those stories about how the world began and the stories about Jesus? Would she ever learn what the black marks meant? Would she ever be able to turn the pages and read the way Father White did?

There was a scuffling by the door and Little Princess looked up to see two girls dressed in long full skirts with white collars around their necks. Their hair was parted in the middle and tied back with a ribbon.

The children stared at Little Princess without speaking. Little Princess stared hard at them until Mistress Margaret Brent crossed the room and said, "Little Princess, here are Caroline and Amelia, wards of our neighbor, Thomas Green."

"Car-o-line. Me-le-a," said Little Princess so slowly that the children laughed and she did too.

Caroline beckoned to her and they all went out into the kitchen. It was a grand, warm, cozy room that smelled just like it looked. Copper pots, long-handled ladles, wooden spoons and long forks hung above the wide fireplace. A large, comfortable looking woman was stirring something in a big, black iron kettle over the low flames.

"This is Martha," Caroline said.

Martha smiled at Little Princess and said, "I expect you are hungry, child. Supper is about ready now."

At supper everybody sat on chairs around the big table and ate roast turkey from pewter plates, with forks. Little Princess had never seen a fork before. She had never sat on a chair before either. It felt funny and made her feet go to sleep to have them hanging down like that.

Governor Calvert sat at one end of the table and Kittamaquund at the other, dressed in English clothes. Kittamaquund had to open his shirt to make room for his strong red neck. His broad shoulders looked broader still in clothes, and his dark face with the black eyes made all the other men look pale as the moon.

Kittamaquund had a hard time holding a fork and finally he gave up trying, picked up his meat and ate it in his fingers.

While they all dined by soft candlelight, the conversation went back and forth across the table, first English then Indian so Kittamaquund could understand. Whenever Little Princess' name was mentioned, she looked up. Eyes often turned her way. They were talking about her in English. What were they saying? She wished she could understand.

Once Father White smiled kindly at her saying in Algonquin, "It won't be long before you will understand."

It was hard to sit still and straight on the chair and listen to words you did not know. Little Princess began to wish that she were home.

After what seemed like a long, long time, she left the table, curled up on the rug in front of the open fire and went to sleep.

While she slept Kittamaquund, Governor Calvert and Mistress Margaret Brent discussed her future. Decisions were made, plans were written down. Finally, papers were signed by Governor Calvert and Mistress Margaret Brent, making Little Princess their ward. They promised in writing to take care of her and educate her jointly.

And Kittamaquund added, "Should anything happen to me, Little Princess is to rule in my place. She is to be Queen of the Pascataway tribe."

It was agreed that everyone would do his best to see that the Emperor's wish was carried out.

Kittamaquund was at peace. His daughter's future was assured. His business in St. Mary's was over and he must return to his people. Now he must leave Little Princess.

He turned to Father White. "This horse my daughter wants, will you ask Governor Calvert to sell him to me?"

So Governor Calvert sold the horse, Big Dog, to Kittamaquund for two hundred beaver skins.

If Little Princess had known what was going on she would have been wide awake.

Kittamaquund stood for some time looking down at the sleeping child. Best to leave at once and spare both himself and her the wound of parting. He turned to Father White saying, "Speak it for me."

The priest raised his hand and said softly, *"Dominus vobiscum."* Kittamaquund nodded, then ran quickly out into the night.

Chapter 11

Big Dog

LITTLE PRINCESS slept all night as soundly as a bear in winter. When she opened her eyes the next morning she found herself in a soft bed with soft warm covers over her and a soft pillow under her head.

She sat up and stretched. As she kicked off the covers Mistress Margaret Brent came in carrying an armful of clothes.

"Good morning," she said looking fresh and vigorous in her own starched dress.

Little Princess said, "Good." She'd forgotten the next word.

"Good *morning*," repeated Mistress Brent.

"Good morn-*ning*."

Mistress Brent smiled and held up a child's linsey-woolsey dress.

Little Princess said, "Me?"

Mistress Brent nodded, "*Dress*. For you."

Little Princess hopped out of bed and began to put on the new clothes. First pantalets with a button, like a small stone, at the waist, then a full petticoat, and last of all the rose-colored dress.

Mistress Brent brushed her straight black hair, braided it and tied it back with a rose-colored ribbon.

Little Princess twirled around and around to show off her skirt. She wished the children at home could see her.

"Now shoes," Mistress Brent said holding out a pair of black leather slippers with a strap.

Little Princess shook her head, "No," and slipped her feet into her own soft moccasins.

"Kittamaquund?" she said. "I will show my dress to my father." She spoke slowly in Algonquin hoping that Mistress Brent would understand. And she did.

"Gone. Gone to Pascataway."

Little Princess looked up at her anxiously. "Gone? Pascataway?"

Mistress Brent nodded and left the room hurriedly.

Little Princess stood still. Her father had gone. At first she was angry. Then she knew why he had left without saying good-by. Good-byes hurt too much. A wave of homesickness swept over her. She didn't want to be left alone in a strange place with strange people.

The door opened again and Caroline and Amelia looked in. They grinned at Little Princess and beckoned to her to come with them.

She held back. They beckoned again, giggling together as if they were up to something. Little Princess was curious. She followed them slowly downstairs, both feet on each step for she had never seen steps before. Down, down, like even rocks on a steep bank. She followed the girls down the hall, through Martha's warm, delicious-smelling kitchen and out the back door.

There was the horse, Big Dog. Martha's boy, Ben, was holding him by the halter.

"Good morn-*ning*, Big Dog," said Little Princess running to him.

The horse swished his tail and pointed his ears.

While Little Princess was stroking his nose, Mistress Brent came outside and said, "The horse is for *you*, Little Princess. Your father bought him for you."

"Big Dog for *me?*" Little Princess could hardly believe it. Caroline and Amelia were laughing, Mistress Brent was nodding and Ben grinned from ear to ear, so it must be so.

Little Princess jumped to hug her horse, scaring him so that he shied, nearly knocking Ben to the ground.

Mistress Brent said, "Come along, children, breakfast is ready."

Caroline and Amelia often came to Sister's Freehold in time for breakfast. They followed Mistress Brent indoors, but Little Princess waited on the step to watch Ben take Big Dog to the stable then she, too, went in with her head full of gay, dancing thoughts.

She had been at St. Mary's for such a short time and already she owned a horse, had two new friends. She knew how to say "come in," "good morning," "for me," "dress," "shoes," and "gone." "Gone" was a sad word. At breakfast she learned to say "pass the biscuits, please." A very happy sentence indeed.

Little Princess expected to spend the rest of the day riding Big Dog, but she didn't for lessons began in the front room as soon as breakfast was over.

The pupils were John, the drummer boy; Caroline and Amelia; Ben, Martha's boy, who tended the cows; and Little Princess. Mistress Margaret Brent was the teacher.

"A, b, c, d. A and b-ab. B and a-ba. C-at, cat." Over and over.

"Window, chair, door. Up, down, under, over." There was so much to learn.

The other children could read and write and everything. They didn't mind sitting still on their chairs. But Little Princess began to twist and squirm. Her new clothes felt itchy. Her belt was too tight. Her mind wandered to the stable and Big Dog. Mistress Brent soon brought it back saying, "Attention, please," in a firm voice. Little Princess did not know what the word "attention" meant but she could guess.

She sat up straight and went back to work, for she wanted to please her teacher. Again, "A, b, c, d," on and on. Now "1, 2, 3, 4, 5, 6." She was glad when the sun was directly overhead and everybody stopped for dinner.

Surely after dinner she would be able to go outdoors with John and Ben. But no. Back to lessons again with Caroline and Amelia. At last when the sun was well on its way down the sky, lessons were over for the day.

Little Princess ran to the stable and found Big Dog cropping grass with the other horses in the field beyond the stable. She wanted to catch him and ride him, but Ben was not in sight and several cows were. She decided to wait until tomorrow.

She climbed up on the fence post and watched Caroline and Amelia as they walked home across the meadow. Once they stopped and waved to her and she waved back. She wished that she were on her way home too.

Later, when it was dark, she longed for her own people. Later still, when she was in bed, the longing went deeper.

The next day everything seemed easier for Little Princess. She did not wriggle quite so much and she

studied her book so well that long before it was time to stop Mistress Brent said, "Good girl. That's enough for today."

In no time Little Princess was outdoors.

Ben caught Big Dog for her and led him close to a stump and held him there while she tried to climb on his back. It wasn't easy for he was a very tall horse. Once she almost made it but Big Dog reared and she landed on the ground.

Little Princess hopped up on the stump and was about to try again when Giles Brent rode around the house on a shiny black horse. He often came over to visit at Sister's Freehold.

"Need some help?" he called out and Ben shouted, "Yes, sir, if you have the time, sir."

Giles tied his horse at the hitching post by the stable and with one swoop he swung Little Princess on to Big Dog's back. Then seeing by her face that she really was frightened, he mounted quickly behind her.

"Good, good," Little Princess said, smiling at him over her shoulder. Then with Giles' arm around her waist to keep her from falling off, she nudged Big Dog with her heels and away they went at a fast trot. Around the house, down the path and up Mattaponi Road as far as Father White's red brick chapel.

On the way back home Giles walked. Little Princess, feeling like the first day of spring, rode alone with her back straight and her knees held in close.

From then on Little Princess rode all over the place. She rode into the town of St. Mary's. It was much larger than Pascataway Village. There were sixty houses there with land between for gardens. Some of them were built of wood like Sister's Freehold, only much smaller. Some were Indian bark houses just like her own home. St. Mary's had been an Indian village at one time. Little Princess had heard about Governor Calvert buying it from the Yaocomicoe, paying cloth, axes, hoes, knives, hatchets, and plows—things the Yaocomicoe could use in their new village.

Someday maybe she would ride out to the end of the road and see if she could find the new village. With a horse of her own she could ride wherever there was a road or a path wide enough for Big Dog.

Chapter 12

PRINCESS MARY OF MARYLAND

THE YEAR passed quickly for Little Princess. On week days there was reading, writing and arithmetic. On Sundays, church. And on Saturdays, play.

Little Princess ran through the deep forest on the far side of the road. She followed rabbit trails. Once she found a fox's nest with three bright-eyed cubs in it. St. Mary's was just like home, with deer, possum, all the same animals and horses too. Little Princess loved to ride horseback. Now she wasn't afraid to catch Big Dog, bridle and saddle him all by herself and go flying down the road on his back.

Often when dark came and the candles were lighted indoors, gentle Mistress Mary Brent taught her to spin, to darn, to knit a sock and turn a neat heel, while Father Fisher read the Bible aloud.

Father White was no longer in St. Mary's. He had gone to Mattaponi to tell the Indians there about Jesus. Father Fisher took his place at St. Mary's Chapel. The

Protestants worshipped in the chapel too. Father White said his chapel was for every faith—not just his own.

Little Princess missed Father White. She missed Kittamaquund and her home. But time passed quickly. Now she knew how to speak English and how to read. If she listened carefully she could even understand the grown people's conversation at the dinner table. She was beginning to know about what was going on outside of Sister's Freehold.

Once when Governor Calvert and Giles Brent were there for dinner she heard Giles say, "There is talk of fighting among the Indians in the north."

"The Susquehannocks," Little Princess put in. "They are mean. They always fight about nothing at all. The Iroquois do too." The men nodded, agreeing. It was good, she thought, to be part of things and not left out.

And once when Governor Calvert said, "Virginia has taken Kent Island by force," she was angry and said, "Kent Island is ours. Virginia cannot keep it." And Governor Calvert said, "It sounds to me as if we have a second Margaret Brent in Maryland."

That pleased Little Princess for Mistress Brent knew what was going on all over the world. Governor Calvert often asked her advice and often took it. Little Princess wanted to grow up to be just like her.

She studied hard, and played hard too.

The following year, when Little Princess was eight years old, sad news came along the Potomac from scout to scout. "Kittamaquund, the Emperor, is dead!"

Her father dead. Little Princess was full of sorrow. Old Indian people died and their bones were gathered together and laid in the earth. Little Princess had seen the round burial mounds of her own tribe. But Kittamaquund was young, strong, and she loved him so.

Her friends tried to comfort her, giving her their sympathy, but it did not help much.

She ran to her room, took off her English clothes and dressed slowly in her own deerskin dress. She thought how her father had shot the deer, how her mother had skinned it, tanned the skin and made the garment for her. Remembering made her sadder still.

She walked through the woods. The trees themselves seemed to mourn for Kittamaquund. Grief was an arrow in her breast.

She walked slowly until she reached the chapel.

"Kittamaquund died a Christian, with his sins forgiven. He is with God," Father Fisher told her.

Little Princess looked at him hopefully. Could it be true?

Little Princess was anxious to become a Christian like her father. She studied harder than ever—English,

Latin, Catechism, Bible, Church History—all of the things that her father wanted her to learn.

Finally, during the winter that Little Princess was nine years old, she was baptized and confirmed in the Roman Catholic Church.

Everybody came to the chapel. The Mistresses Brent, Governor Calvert, all of the members of the assembly, Thomas Green, Caroline and Amelia, his wards, were there, and the drummer boy and Ben. Everybody was dressed in his Sunday best. The church itself was filled with evergreen boughs and holly. But all eyes were on Little Princess, dressed in a white dress trimmed with lace, made especially for her by Mistress Mary Brent.

It was a solemn and wonderful occasion. Little Princess' heart was full and light. And at the end of the ceremony, while she was still on her knees, Father Fisher said, "You will be called Mary, after the mother of Jesus."

"And after Mistress Mary too," thought Little Princess proudly.

"Mary." Such a pretty name. If only Father White were there, and Kittamaquund! Perhaps Kittamaquund was there. No one knows the ways of heaven.

Going home from church while they were all walking along together, Mistress Margaret Brent said to the new Mary, "First you were called Little Girl, then

Little Princess, and now you are Princess Mary of Maryland. What next?"

And Giles walking behind answered, "Next she will be Queen of the Pascataways."

But Princess Mary said, "Next I go home."

Chapter 13

GILES BRENT

*P*RINCESS MARY of Maryland, a good, good name, but the Princess herself liked to be called plain Mary.

Mary did not go home as she planned. Spring was just beginning to stir in Maryland when bad news reached St. Mary's. A Pascataway scout told the news to the scout from Potopaco and he in turn told the scout from St. Clements and he told the look-out scout from St. Mary's and he ran swiftly to Sister's Freehold.

"The Susquehannocks and the Iroquois are on the warpath," he said. "Villages along the rivers are in peril. Travel is dangerous."

Father Fisher prayed, "Oh, Lord, we beseech Thee to crush the pride of our enemies and humble their stubborn wills by the might of Thy hand."

The people answered, "Amen."

Later, when the wild cherry trees looked like brides, more news reached St. Mary's. A scout told a scout and on down the river came the message, "The Susquehannocks have retreated for a time. Be wary still. Best not travel for a moon or two."

Then still more news came along, "The Pascataway tribe, loyal to the Emperor Kittamaquund when he was alive, now disregard his wish to have his daughter rule after him. Instead they have elected the brave, Weghucasso, to rule."

When Mistress Margaret Brent heard that Mary would not be Queen, she said to Governor Calvert, "The night that Mary became our ward we heard Kittamaquund claim her as his heir. We must do all we can to see that his wish is carried out."

Giles Brent said, "Yes. If Mary were ruler of the Pascataways she would own more land and tobacco than any other woman in Maryland. As Queen she would see to it that her tribes would protect St. Mary's against the hostile tribes."

Governor Calvert agreed but he had no time for Indian affairs now. He was a very busy man. There were many changes taking place in Maryland. Laws had to be enforced. New laws had to be made. The colony was growing. Claiborne, the Virginian, was making trouble at Kent Island. In England, Parliament rose up against the King over colonial affairs. Of course, Marylanders were loyal to their king.

There were changes at Sister's Freehold too.

John, the drummer boy, had left to join the Kent Island troops under Captain Giles Brent.

Ben, the boy who tended the cows, had gone to work as farmer on Giles Brent's estate.

Caroline and Amelia, their studies finished, were helping Father Fisher in the parish school for young children.

That left Mary the only pupil with three able teachers.

Mary always was a good student. Now that there were no other children to say, "Let's go out and play," she was better still.

Penmanship: Quill held firmly, strokes even, up to the right, down left. Keep on the line.

Arithmetic: If one cow gives milk for six people, how many cows are required to feed thirty-five people? Easy—six cows with cream enough left over for three cats. Arithmetic was fun.

Geography: Maps showing the whole world. "What a big ocean to cross in the *Ark* and the *Dove*. And all of England not much bigger than Kent Island. How clever of Captain John Smith to put Pascataway Village on his map."

History: Queen Elizabeth, then James the First, and

now Charles the First, ruling England. Mary learned most about England from Martha. Often she would wipe supper dishes and while Martha worked she would tell Mary about the old days in England when the Brents lived in a big house.

"Tell about parties," Mary would say. And Martha would talk until Mary could hear the music and see the lords and ladies whirling round and round the great hall in their lovely clothes, colored like the rainbow.

There was so much to learn. Languages too. French and Spanish from Mistress Brent. Later, Greek with Father Fisher.

And don't forget the gracious everyday business of being a lady, with its curtsey, its "How do you do," "I beg your pardon," and "After you."

And elocution: "Drink to me only with thine eyes." Poems by the dozen from memory.

Needlepoint, drawing, music and dancing.

Whenever Giles Brent stopped at Sister's Freehold he would say, "Play for me, Mary." And Mary would play the harpsichord and sing for him.

Whenever Father Fisher, Governor Calvert or Giles Brent stopped in for a visit, Mary took part in the conversation.

Once when Governor Calvert said over a mug of hot cider, "Maryland is losing Kent Island; we cannot hold out much longer against Claiborne." Mary, her black eyes flashing with anger, said, "Then fight. How dare anybody take away one single bit of our Maryland?"

At that the men laughed and Governor Calvert called her "a savage, still." Then he added soberly, "You are right, Mary. It is time to fight but we do not have enough men."

Whereupon Mistress Brent suggested that he go to England and get help. The Governor nodded. A good idea and a timely one, for recently his brother, Lord Baltimore, had sent for him to return to England for a visit. Yes, he would go and while there he would ask for men.

He turned to Giles Brent, "While I am away, Giles, I appoint you to act as governor of Maryland."

Giles was pleased. He was an able man with two able sisters to guide him.

Captain Giles Brent was commander of the Kent Island troops, owner of sixty acres of town land, one thousand acres of wilderness land on Kent Island and co-owner with Mistress Margaret Brent of two thousand acres more on the other side of the river. Giles was an ambitious man. It pleased him to be acting-governor of Maryland, a position of highest rank.

Before long Governor Calvert sailed to England, knowing that Maryland would be well governed in his absence. And it was. Giles was a hard worker, faithful and trustworthy, but he wanted more land and tobacco. For land was money.

What about all that land left to Mary by her father?

Yes, what about it? The more Giles thought on the subject the more interested he became.

One night after Mary had gone to bed he went over to Sister's Freehold. His sisters were knitting by candle-light. They looked up when he entered the room.

"I've been thinking about Mary a great deal lately," he said, getting right to the point. "If I were to marry her while I am governor, I might be able to claim the inheritance for her."

"Marry Mary! Why, she's only a child," the two women said together. "And you are thirty-eight."

Giles brushed that thought aside saying, "Many young women are married in England at her age and I'll wager that all Indian girls marry earlier still."

"Mary is my ward, don't forget," Mistress Margaret stated firmly. "Are you thinking of her welfare or your own?"

"I am fond of Mary. I am able to take care of her as you well know." With that he turned on his heel and left the house before more could be said.

He'd stop over and see Mary after lunch the next day.

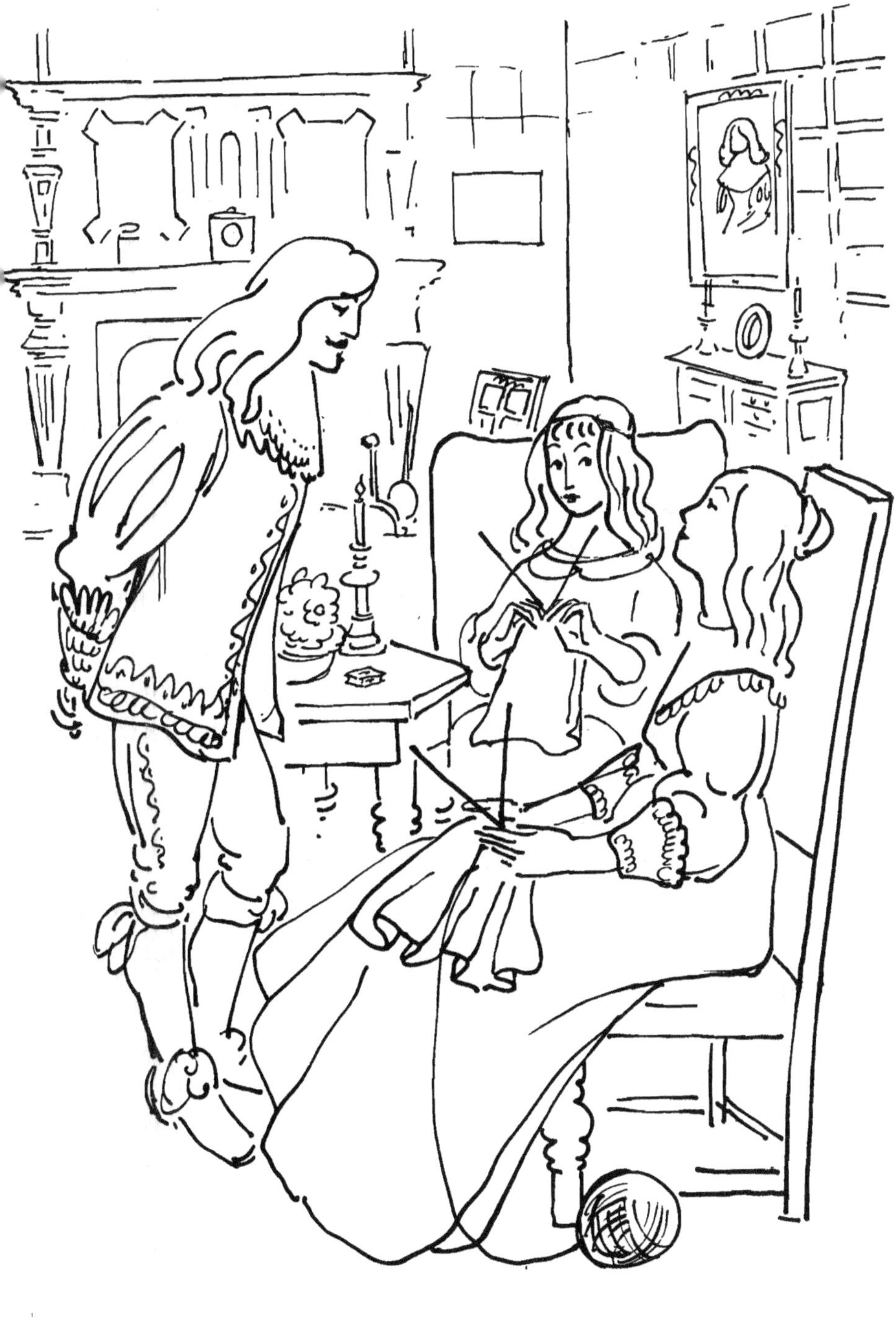

But he didn't. For early in the morning while Giles was in Governor Calvert's office loking over some important papers, a messenger arrived.

"A ship is entering the harbor, sir," he said. "The *Reformation*, sir, under Captain Ingle, one of Claiborne's men."

"He comes for a cargo of corn and tobacco," said Giles without looking up from his work. "Let me know when Captain Ingle comes ashore. I will go and greet him."

The messenger ran out and returned within the hour. He was quite breathless.

"The ship, sir. She lies at anchor now and our men say that Ingle speaks loudly against the King."

Giles jumped to his feet, "Throw him in irons. *We* are loyal supporters of the King. Throw him in irons and his men with him."

The messenger ran to carry out the order.

Giles didn't have time to think of Mary.

And at supper Mary had a hard time keeping up with the table talk. It went back and forth, fast, and there was anger in it.

She listened without saying a word. As soon as supper was over, she saddled Big Dog and rode fast to the chapel to tell Father Fisher the news. It was almost dark and everything was still. There was not a sound except the thud, thud of Big Dog's hooves as he trotted along Mattaponi Road. As soon as they reached the chapel Mary tied Big Dog to the hitching rail and went inside.

When Father Fisher heard about Ingle and the ship he said, "I will ride back to Sister's Freehold with you, Mary. I must hear more about this."

When they came out of the chapel together Big Dog was not there.

"What could have happened to him, Father Fisher?" exclaimed Mary. "I left him *right here* a few minutes ago."

"Perhaps his rein loosened. He may have returned

to his own stable. Come along and we will find him."

Mary took Father Fisher's hand and the two of them walked fast to Sister's Freehold.

Big Dog was not in his stable. Ben had not seen him. No one had.

Before long news reached Sister's Freehold that one of Ingle's men from the ship had escaped. There had been a thorough search for him and he was not in St. Mary's. He had not left by canoe, for the harbor was closely watched.

Now Mary was angry. "He took my horse," she said with her eyes flashing. "He took Big Dog and rode away on him. I know he did."

Giles told her not to worry. "We have their ship, don't forget. I will demand that the horse be returned."

Mary looked up at him saying, "I hope the man feeds Big Dog and gives him plenty of water."

Giles gave the order for the horse to be returned at once. But two days passed and there was no sign of Big Dog.

The following night, while everybody in St. Mary's was asleep, the ship *Reformation* pulled anchor and sailed away with Ingle aboard.

"Claiborne himself must have come," Giles said. But no one ever found out just what happened.

Time went on and it began to look as if Mary had lost Big Dog forever. She was sad, but deep down she felt that some day she would see him again.

Chapter 14

MARY KITTAMAQUUND BRENT

A FEW DAYS later Giles stopped at Sister's Freehold in time for lunch. Mary ran to meet him. She wore a sprigged linsey-woolsey dress. Her black hair was as shiny as satin and she wore her blue beads, for she was going calling on the sick with Father Fisher later in the day.

"Oh, Uncle Giles," she said, "see my needlepoint." She held out a footstool cover with roses neatly stitched against black. "Aunt Mary says I sew as well as a grown woman."

"You are almost a grown woman, Mary, and don't call me *Uncle*," Giles said smiling at her.

Quickly she curtseyed, holding out her skirt and to tease she said, "I beg your pardon, Honorable Governor."

He laughed heartily. "You mock me, Mary. I wish that you would call me Giles."

Mary looked up at him. He was tall and handsome. She held out her hand, curtseying again in her best Sunday manner, saying, "How do you do, Giles."

He bowed, took her hand, raised it high and off they went, dancing the gavotte in double time; two short jumps to the right, two short jumps to the left, turn, a kiss on the cheek and off again.

It was such fun to be grown up, to dance with a grown man. Mary imagined herself at the Governor's Ball, all dressed up in satin and silk, dancing with Giles. But never did she dream of a wedding.

When, a moment later, Giles said, "Mary, I want you to be my wife," she stopped dancing, let go of his hand and ran out into the hall where she bumped square into Mistress Margaret Brent.

"Oh, Aunt Margaret," Mary exclaimed with excitement, "Giles just asked me to *marry* him."

"And you, Mary, what was your answer?" Mistress Brent wanted to know.

Mary turned and looked at Giles standing across the room by the window. She ran to him quickly saying, "I say yes, yes, *yes*."

It wasn't long before St. Mary's was buzzing with the news. Sister's Freehold was turned upside down. Martha was hustling back and forth, getting out the best china, polishing andirons, shining silver, getting ready for the wedding.

Mistress Mary was busy sewing. Mistress Margaret, too, stitched late by candlelight, for Mary must have lots of pretty clothes.

Mistress Mary, Mistress Margaret and Giles all agreed that Mary was to wear their mother's wedding gown. And so the leather trunk was hauled out of the storage closet and the lovely, white satin dress was tenderly lifted from the box where it had been so carefully packed away.

How beautiful it was with its soft full skirt, the bodice with long sleeves edged in lace, as delicate as a spider's web. Mary felt like a queen when she tried on the wedding dress.

"Stand still, child, while I fit the waist." It was a bit too tight. Mistress Mary's expert needle would soon ease it.

Mary, happy and excited, dashed from one thing to another like a dragonfly, with her head full of dreams.

If only Kittamaquund, Father White and Big Dog were there.

News of the wedding had been sent to Pascataway Village. Nicoatucen would come and Mosorcoques, perhaps, but not her mother. There were two small sisters now; her mother must stay with them. Some day after they were married Giles would take Mary to Pascataway to visit her people.

Mary awoke at dawn on her wedding day. She ran outdoors in her bare feet and picked a great armful of flowers—goldenrod, asters and black-eyed Susans. Some for the house, some for the chapel and some for the bride.

Long before it was time for the wedding, the chapel was full of people. Everybody in St. Mary's was there and visitors from Pascataway, Potopaco and Mattaponi —not Father White, for he had gone back to England.

Mary was so excited that she never knew how she reached the altar all in one piece. But there she was in the lovely wedding dress, with Giles beside her. And Father Fisher married them in the presence of God, all the angels and all of the good people gathered in the chapel.

Then Mary Kittamaquund Brent, first lady of Maryland, walked down the aisle on the arm of her husband, Giles.

As soon as they were outside of the chapel door Mary exclaimed, "Look, Giles, look there! It's Big Dog. See him?"

Sure enough, Big Dog, fat and shiny, was standing at the hitching rail with the other horses.

Mary ran to him, her gown trailing across the grass.

"Big Dog, you are safe and sound and home again. I am
so glad you came to my wedding."

Big Dog whinnied and pointed his ears.

By now the people were coming out of the chapel.
They gathered around to congratulate the bride and
groom.

Before long Giles found out all about Big Dog. How
an Indian from Mattaponi had found him wandering
along the river near the town and how he had kept him
for his own and had ridden him to the wedding.

"But he is *mine*," said Mary.

Surely no one could resist Mary on her wedding day,

least of all Giles. He traded one of his own best horses for Big Dog.

"Lift me on his back," said Mary, now all smiles.

Giles swung her into the saddle, wedding dress and all. And Mary Kittamaquund Brent rode home. Big Dog must have felt the dignity of the occasion for he did not trot but walked all the way and Giles walked beside him.

Mistress Margaret Brent, Mistress Mary, Father Fisher and all of the guests followed, for there was a big party at Sister's Freehold that day. Everybody came to drink a toast to the bride and groom.

For some time Giles tried his best to claim the title of Queen for his bride. He failed, but he found something much better. He fell in love with Mary and she fell in love with him.

And when Governor Calvert returned from England, Giles helped him take Kent Island back from Claiborne of Virginia.

Then Giles took his bride across the river to his beautiful place called "Peace" in Virginia where he built a fine, large house for her. There was a wing for Mistress Margaret and Mistress Mary and a room for Martha and four extra bedrooms. There was a stable, too, for Big Dog and the other horses, barns for cows and chickens, sheds for sheep and pens for hogs.

It was a good thing that Giles built a large house with extra rooms for it wasn't long before there were children in the family—a boy, Giles, and a girl, Mary. And later, to the delight of everybody, there was a new baby —Richard.

In winter the children played on the wide stairway and learned to make cookies in Martha's kitchen. They built castles with their blocks and played "catchers," shouting and laughing as they raced down the long halls.

In summer the children climbed trees, swam in the river and played games on the lawn.

Every day when the swallows began to circle the woods at sundown, Mary read the Bible aloud to her family or told a story.

What a picture they made. Giles smoking his pipe with his setter dog asleep at his feet and Mary sitting in a big chair with the baby on her lap and the other children gathered around her. Young Mary was wearing a string of blue beads around her neck, and young Giles held a worn Indian doll in his arms.

"Tell us a story, Mother."

"What shall it be? The Good Samaritan? The Prodigal Son?"

"Tell us the story of Princess Mary of Maryland."

"Yes, yes, Princess Mary."

Mary had told the story many times for she wanted her children to know Kittamaquund, Father White, and all the wonderful people she had known. She wanted them to know Maryland, its forests, its rivers, birds and animals. She looked over at Giles. Dear Giles. Then she began,

"A long time ago in Pascataway Village, high on a bluff overlooking the water, there lived a *anishee-nabie-equay-enss.*"

"A little Indian girl," the children said together, "and her name was Little Girl. Go on, Mother. Tell the rest."

The baby went to sleep. The swallows went to rest. An owl hooted off in the woods and the moon rose up behind the trees before Princess Mary of Maryland came to the end of her story.

Nan Hayden Agle was born and grew up in Catonsville, Maryland, where her family lived in an old stone house built in 1732. Mrs. Agle's mother was an artist and Nan Agle says, "Our house was large and we had lots of company—artists, writers and dancers, because they could do as they pleased and there was always plenty to eat."

Mrs. Agle has always liked to draw and to write. She is on the teaching staff of the Baltimore Museum of Art, and—with Ellen Wilson—has written THREE BOYS AND A TRAIN, THREE BOYS AND A MINE, THREE BOYS AND A TUGBOAT, THREE BOYS AND A LIGHTHOUSE, and THREE BOYS AND THE REMARKABLE COW.

CPSIA information can be obtained
at www.ICGtesting.com
Printed in the USA
FSHW01n1956310718
51065FS